Architectural Design

The New Mix
Culturally Dynamic Architecture

Guest-edited by Sara Caples and Everardo Jefferson

 WILEY-ACADEMY

Architectural Design
Vol 75 No 5 Sept/Oct 2005

Editorial Offices
International House
Ealing Broadway Centre
London W5 5DB
T: +44 (0)20 8326 3800
F: +44 (0)20 8326 3801
E: architecturaldesign@wiley.co.uk

Editor
Helen Castle

Editorial and Production Management
Mariangela Palazzi-Williams

Art Direction/Design
Christian Küsters (CHK Design)

Design Assistant
Hannah Dumphy (CHK Design)

**Project Coordinator
and Picture Editor**
Caroline Ellerby

Advertisement Sales
Faith Pidduck/Wayne Frost
01243 770254
fpidduck@wiley.co.uk

Editorial Board
Will Alsop, Denise Bratton, Adriaan
Beukers, André Chaszar, Peter Cook,
Teddy Cruz, Max Fordham, Massimiliano
Fuksas, Edwin Heathcote, Anthony Hunt,
Charles Jencks, Jan Kaplicky, Robert
Maxwell, Jayne Merkel, Monica Pidgeon,
Antoine Predock, Michael Rotondi, Leon
van Schaik, Ken Yeang

Contributing Editors
André Chaszar
Craig Kellogg
Jeremy Melvin
Jayne Merkel

ISBN 0470014679

Profile No 177

Front cover: Queens Theatre-in-the-Park, Flushing Meadows Park, Queens, New York. Original building: New York State Pavilion by Philip Johnson, 1964. Extension by Caples Jefferson Architects, 2005. Cover design © Caples Jefferson Architects, Rendering © Cicada Design.

Abbreviated positions:
b=bottom, c=centre, l=left, r=right

Ⅾ
p 4 © Sue Barr; p 5 © Albert Vecerka/ESTO; p 6(t) © Martti Kapanen, Alvar Aalto Museum; p 6(bl) © Renzo Piano Building Workshop, photo William Vassal; p 6(br) © Herzog & de Meuron; p 7 © Paul Raftery/VIEW; pp 8-11 © Sue Barr; p 12 © Will Alsop Architects; p 13 © John Burrell; p 14(t) © Greenhill Jenner Architects, photos Charlotte Wood Photography; p 14(c&b) © Greenhill Jenner Architects; pp 16-22 © Julian Olivas; p23 © Cicada Design Inc, Toronto, Canada; pp 24 & 27(b) © Melanie Taylor, lighting designer, NBBJ; p 26(t) © Jamie Horwitz; pp 26(b) & 27(t) courtesy OMA; p 28(t) © Mikesch Muecke; pp 28(b) & 29 courtesy Peter Walker and Partners; pp 30-31 © Anton Grassi; pp 32-37 © Teddy Cruz, Jose Jaime Samper & Giacomo Castagnola; pp 38-39 & 43 © David Goldblatt; p 40 © Harber Masson and Associates; pp 41(t&b) © Brian Verwey; p 41(c) © Sadiq Toffa; p 42 © Heather Dodd; pp 44-47 & 48(b) © Cengiz Bektas; pp 48(t) & 49 © Nevzat Sayin; pp 50 & 54© Amit Cohen and Sagi Shuali; pp 51 & 52(main) © Ruth Palmon; pp 52(insert) & 53 © Ahikam Seri; pp 55, 57(t) & 58-61 © Anooradha Iyer Siddiqi; p 56 © Kerstin Park-Laballa; p 57(b) © SN & NN Kanade, photo NN Kanade; pp 62, 66(b) & 67-68 © Architect Hafeez Contractor; p 63(t&cr) © Kazi Ashraf; pp 63 (b&cl), 64(t) & 65(c) © Rajeev Kathpalia, Ahmedabad, India; p 64(c) © Md Rafiq Azam, photo Shafiqul Alam; p 64(b) © Shakeel Hossain; p 65(l) Ram Rahman; p 65(tr) © Uttam Kumar Saha; p 65(br) © Kashef Chowdhury; p 66(t) courtesy Rajshri Productions, 2003; pp 70-77 © Edward Denison; pp 78-80, 81(b) & 82-83 © Steven Holl Architects; p 81(t) © Andy Ryan; pp 84-85 & 88(t) © Earl Carter; p 86(t) © Terroir Pty Ltd; p 86(b) © Greg Burgess Architects, photo Jimmy Yang; p 87(t) © Nicholas Murray, Melissa Bright, Kirstan Grant, Shelley Freeman, Jonathon Podborsek, Hannah Mathews; p 87(c&b) © John Gollings; p 88(c) © Daniël Van Cleemput, photo John Gollings; p 88(b) Daniël Van Cleemput; p 89(t) © Kerry Hill/Albert Lim KS; p 89(ct) © Look Architects; p 89(cb) © Ivan Rijavec, photos John Gollings; p 89(b) © WOHA; p 90(t) © Lyons Architects, photo John Gollings; p 90(c) Kerstin Thompson Architects, photo Jeremy Addison; p 90(b) © John Gollings; p 92 © Society for the Preservation of Weeksville and Bedford-Stuyvesant History; p 93(t) © Jean-Paul Bourdier; pp 93(c&b) & 95-95© Caples Jefferson Architects.

Ⅾ+
pp 98-101 © MGM Mirage; pp 102-104 © Peter Durant; pp 105-106 © MacCormac Jamieson Prichard; pp 107, 108(t&b), 110-111, 112(b) & 113-114 © Hodgetts+Fung Design and Architecture; p 108(c) © Benny Chan/Fotoworks; p 112(t) © Lara Swimmer/ESTO; pp 115-117 © Page + Park Architects; pp 120-121 © Ian Abley, www.audacity.org; p 122(t) © Airlight Ltd; p 122(b) © John-Paul Frazer & Jacques Abelman; p 123 © Tachi Laboratory, University of Tokyo; p 124 © Ateliers Jean Nouvel; pp 125 & 126(t&c) © Rafael Vargas.

Subscription Offices UK
John Wiley & Sons Ltd.
Journals Administration Department
1 Oldlands Way, Bognor Regis
West Sussex, PO22 9SA
T: +44 (0)1243 843272
F: +44 (0)1243 843232
E: cs-journals@wiley.co.uk

Printed in Italy by Conti Tipicolor.
All prices are subject to change
without notice.
[ISSN: 0003-8504]

Ⅾ is published bimonthly and is available to purchase on both a subscription basis and as individual volumes at the following prices.

Single Issues
Single issues UK: £22.50
Singles issues outside UK: US$45.00
Details of postage and packing charges available on request.

Annual Subscription Rates 2005
Institutional Rate
Print only or Online only: UK£175/US$290
Combined Print and Online: UK£193/US$320
Personal Rate
Print only: UK£99/US$155
Student Rate
Print only: UK£70/US$110

Prices are for six issues and include postage and handling charges. Periodicals postage paid at Jamaica, NY 11431. Air freight and mailing in the USA by Publications Expediting Services Inc, 200 Meacham Avenue, Elmont, NY 11003

Individual rate subscriptions must be paid by personal cheque or credit card. Individual rate subscriptions may not be resold or used as library copies.

Postmaster
Send address changes to Ⅾ Publications Expediting Services, 200 Meacham Avenue, Elmont, NY 11003

4	Editorial *Helen Castle*
5	Introduction: Mixology *Sara Caples + Everardo Jefferson*
8	London Calling *Jeremy Melvin*
16	Crazy Quilt Queens *Jayne Merkel*
24	Fabricating Pluralism *Jamie Horwitz*
32	Tijuana Case Study – Tactics of Invasion: Manufactured Sites *Teddy Cruz*
38	House/Home: Dwelling in the New South Africa *Iain Low*
44	Cengiz Bektas and the Community of Kuzguncuk in Istanbul *David Height*
50	Building Traditions: The Benny W Reich Cultural Center for the Ethiopian Community, Yavneh, Israel *Ruth Palmon*
55	Making Place in Bangalore *Anooradha Iyer Siddiqi*
62	Masala City: Urban Stories from South Asia *Kazi K Ashraf*
70	Twenty-First Century China *Edmund Ong*
78	Holl on Hybrids *Everardo Jefferson*
84	Australasia *Leon Van Schaik*
91	Weeksville Education Building *Sara Caples*

The New Mix:
Culturally Dynamic Architecture
Guest-edited by Sara Caples and Everardo Jefferson

98+	Interior Eye: Turning Japanese *Craig Kellogg*
102+	Building Profile: Senior Common Room Extension, St John's College, Oxford *Jeremy Melvin*
107+	Practice Profile: Hodgetts+Fung: The Art of Remix *Denise Bratton*
115+	Home Run: Westerton Road, Grangemouth *Henry McKeown*
119+	Book Review: Expressing More Than Structure *Kate and Ian Abley*
122+	McLean's Nuggets *Will McLean*
124+	Site Lines: Puerta of Dreams *Howard Watson*

Brick Lane, London, 2005.

As I write this editorial at the end of July 2005, this issue of AD has a poignancy that was never anticipated at its inception. In light of the London bombings, there is a strong awareness that the costs for a society of a culture that does not realise true diversity and dynamic interaction may just be too high. True multiculturalism in the arts, however, should not be realised in a sense of political expediency. It cannot be paid lip service as a convenient flash-in-the-pan government policy. It requires the excitement and enduring energy of committed designers and artists. The guest-editors of this publication, Sara Caples and Everardo Jefferson, are such architects. They set up their practice, Caples Jefferson Architects, in New York almost two decades ago, and since then have been working with communities in the city on public building and nonprofit projects. Their unswerving commitment to the non-commercial sector has paid off, as in the last few years they have been awarded nationally by their peers. What, however, is remarkable, is the fact that despite the uphill struggle of often working to the tight budgets of charitable foundations and city authorities, their enthusiasm has not waivered. This issue is testimony to that fact, as they have set out to explore the possibilities of a rich vein of culturally absorbent Modernism, while also acknowledging the need to employ the highly contemporary modes of 'quick switching, layering and reframing'. In this volume, Caples and Jefferson have stretched out to a global network of people with similar preoccupations. Most impressively, those such as Teddy Cruz in San Diego and Cengiz Bektas in Istanbul have also made a vocation of transversing cultures. This is also underscored by research into local contexts, which take in New York, London, South Africa, Bangalore in southern India, China and Australia. In △+, LA-based architects Hodgetts+Fung, with their invocation of 'the art of the remix', make an interesting postscript to the opportunities that the 'new mix' can offer. △

MIXOLOGY

Caples Jefferson Architects with artist Nathan Slate Joseph, Heritage Health and Housing headquarters, New York, 2001
A patchwork of 'Hispanic' colours clads the facade.

What is the New Mix in architecture? Why is it emerging now? Is there a direct correlation between the widening of the ethnic origins of practitioners and diversity in design? What are the impacts on the formal language of architecture? Sara Caples and Everardo Jefferson consider issues related to mixology, defined by the *American Heritage Dictionary* as 'the study or skill of preparing mixed drinks'.

We are indeed at a time when many cultures embrace the concept of 'modern' as representative of themselves. As more places develop cutting-edge technologies, create conditions of improved social justice, and rush to build explosively growing cities, 'modern' embodies deep aspirations.

A second condition of the present is that the indigenous culture of most large cities is increasingly a mix – ethnically diverse, encompassing customs, colours, flavours, dreamlike visions of many different origins.

The desire to embrace this dynamic of cultural broadening compels many architects to consider ways of extending the compass of Modernism to create an architecture truly representative of a wider range of humanity.

This condition of mixing cultures is not always comfortable. Sometimes, especially within immigrant communities, the existence of cultural dynamism first manifests itself in modest signs only – shop signs or shop window displays – while appropriating the pre-existing context as a protective cloak. On the other hand, explosively embraced visions of the future sometimes lead to fantastic new creations of questionable taste, theme-park visions of modern crossed with heritage. Yet the impulse to bridge cultures can also lead to representative works treasured by their communities and, at its best, to a vision of a hybrid art pointing to architecture's future.

Alvar Aalto, Villa Mairea, Noormarkku, Finland, 1938–41
The language of Modernism is extended to evoke the forests of Finland.

A rising group of practitioners is meeting the challenge of this broadening cultural landscape. Unsurprisingly, many of the architects exploring multiple cultures in architecture are themselves either constant travellers or immigrants, insiders/outsiders. They understand that the new traveller-immigrant is not aspiring to replace one culture with another, but, rather, pursuing strategies of quick switching, layering and reframing – strategies requiring knowledge, mental flexibility and, occasionally, not a little humour.

This issue showcases the work of a number of firms that have made multiplicity of perspectives a basal condition of their thinking. The new 'multiculture' demands strategies capable of dealing with contradictory impulses – an openness to hybrids. Hence, contrast, morphing and fusion are characteristic of an architecture that attempts to capture layered Gestalts, perceptual patterns and structures that resonate for a broadened range of humanity.

Working as we do at the intersection of several cultures, we have been on the lookout for signs of this dynamic culture in architecture and are increasingly coming across the work of

Renzo Piano Building Workshop, Jean-Marie Tjibaou Cultural Center, Nouméa, New Caledonia, 1991–8
'Huts' interpreting traditional Kanak housing shelter cultural and administrative functions of the centre.

practitioners exploring this new reality. Sometimes the work is by architects such as Teddy Cruz in San Diego, compelled by their ethnicity to look beyond the mainstream. And sometimes the work is a reframing, based on the concept of multiple cultures coexisting in a single place, such as Herzog & de Meuron's De Young Museum in San Francisco, where the texture of the spaces is intentionally varied in order to sympathetically display artefacts from a wide range of ethnic origins.

These architectural expressions of multiple cultures are not repudiations of Modernism; rather, they represent an enrichment that may ultimately help to create a more robust Modernism, helping to rescue it from the blight of too much sameness. Architects such as the Kanade brothers, with their roof gardens in Bangalore (see 'Making Place in Bangalore'), and Ilan Pivko, with his concrete 'mud' Ethiopian community centre in Israel (see 'Building Traditions') are creating fusions of treasured images and modern tectonics.

Such developments are giving rise to a Modern architecture that is broader in its intentions and, ultimately, one that values heterogeneity and the fantastic variety of human creativity.

Modernism: A Clean Broom at Its Roots

A core impulse of Modernism is that of being stripped down, antimonumental, without style. The idea of throwing out old images is particularly appealing within formerly imperial or colonised cultures where the past may confer much psychic baggage. Modernism is seen as a new beginning, a step towards a better future, clean of oppressive ideologies.

Yet by the 1920s, some architects began to introduce an emotive range back into the fabric of Modern architecture. There is a line of Expressionism from Mendelsohn through Scharoun, and Saarinen to Gehry, to the present 'blob' explorations. Another way of extending this range has been to look to a broader range of cultures, whether through Alvar Aalto's evocation of Finnish forests at Villa Mairea, or Le Corbusier's borrowing from African art-forms for Ronchamp. It is this rich vein that *The New Mix* wishes to explore.

Herzog & de Meuron, Fröhlich House, Stuttgart, Germany 1995
A child's vision of a house rendered in glass and wooden cladding.

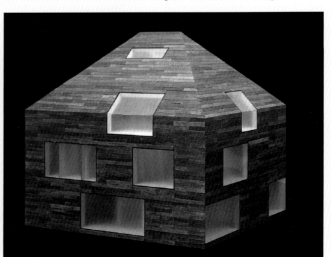

Enric Miralles (EMBT/RMJM), Scottish Parliament, Edinburgh, 2004
The austere energies of the Scottish city captured and released.

If Modernism is a reaction to earlier eclectic 'themed' buildings like Barry and Pugin's 'Gothic' Houses of Parliament (1835–60) and Garnier's floridly detailed Paris Opéra (1857–74), and, further, as many current practitioners consider late 20th-century Postmodernism a failed experiment in borrowed iconography, how can architects incorporate a broader range of cultures into Modernism without resorting to pastiche?

We have avoided using the word tradition because it implies copying as opposed to deeper interpretations. It is not a question of being representational through the back door, but rather of channelling information streams of cultural traditions, spatial imprints, materiality, landscape and colours into Modern architecture.

Culture is incremental, added to by successive generations, uniquely reinterpreted from one individual to another, so we are not usually describing a revolution, but more a series of hybrids – tentative, ambiguous, unorthodox, interesting, perhaps finding validity in formerly dismissed cultures.

Ingredients in the Mix

We do not actually subscribe to the idea that architecture can be created from a recipe. We see the design process as iterative and didactic, albeit using intuitively derived elements. Hybridisation requires combining pieces and layers to make a whole – it takes a lot of art to create something coherent. But you have to begin somewhere, so it might be useful here to discuss a few of the elements a hybrid work might contain.

At the heart is the process of abstracting culturally representational elements. At its most basic, this might be *a parti* like Herzog & de Meuron's simplification of a traditional Swiss house into a form that resembles a child's drawing of a ridged box, pierced by an eerie pattern of glazed openings, surprising the viewer by juxtaposing a known symbol of home with unexpected passages.

Culturally distinct forms can layer on as iconic form-givers; for example, Renzo Piano's New Caledonia cultural centre, with its great arcing screens of wood providing cooling shade and proclaiming identity derived from traditional Kanak building forms.

Materiality and constructional methods hold great associative power, linked as they often are to specific places. Reinhold Martin's definition of material as a nature/culture hybrid reminds us of this cultural power, manifested in such works as Peter Zumthor's wooden chapel at Sogn Benedegt, in Switzerland.

Colours are a subject in themselves, as associations differ radically from culture to culture. The same white that is perceived as 'pure' in the West is emblematic of mourning elsewhere; whereas red, with its associations of passion and rage in puritan societies, is the colour of celebration and joy to others. A case in point is our Heritage headquarters facade, which was originally designed in greens and blues only, until our clients told us that such a palette was too 'downtown' and needed strong reds and yellows to appeal to their mostly Hispanic clients.

While modern practitioners may still consider ornament a sin, collaboration with artists can be a very productive way to broaden the cultural reach of a place. Gehry's work famously benefited from collaborations with Claes Oldenburg and Richard Serra. In this issue, Nicolas Murray's multimedia work, described in 'Australasia', points to the wider range of psychological exploration opened up by combining art with architecture.

Landscape is, historically, at least as culturally dynamic as buildings. Native plant forms are constantly challenged by imports like the eucalyptus forests along the formerly arid coasts of Southern California. Because landscape is so incrementally malleable, it is often a first site of cultural transformations. And as the 'green' agenda grows increasingly important, reconsideration of porosity, modulation of light and materiality can be broadened by consulting a wider range of cultural strategies from channelling wind through directive roof structures, to thickening walls to absorb heat, to using locally extracted materials to minimise processing and transportation.

Organisational and programmatic particularities can inform a project. Beyond the obvious sensitivities, as in the separate entrances for men and women required by some Asian communites (see 'London Calling'), more subtle interpretations offer great richness, as in the Fukuoka housing project where Steven Holl transmutes the sliding walls of Japanese space into folding hinged planes within the apartments (see 'Holl on Hybrids'). The relationship of open to closed, of light and shade, can be enriched. The portico of Richard Rogers Partnership's Carré d'Art building in Nîmes derives its identity directly from the adjacent Maison Carrée, even if the rest of the building cheerfully ignores ancient spatial attitudes. As Iain Low points out in his article on South African housing, introducing different patterns of density and social organisation can enhance the urbanisation of cities that must be more effectively shared.

A rich hybrid will combine many of these elements in a way that preserves the coherence of their origins, yet builds to something more. At its best, the process of hybridising, married to the sensitivities of a gifted architect, can result in a powerful work of architecture, such as Enric Miralles' parliament building in Edinburgh, with its haunting response to the grey stone of the Scottish city.

At their most effective, these architectural transformations can go beyond collaging, deeper than narrative, touching not just the surfaces of a culture, but reaching beyond. Something else happening.

That's what makes it so difficult. And so rewarding. ∆

LONDON CALLING

An ethnic mix has always been an essential part of London's character, with areas such as Spitalfields home to successive waves of immigrants — from Huguenots in the 18th century to a diverse Jewish population in the mid-20th century, and a sizable Bangladeshi community today. **Jeremy Melvin** explains how, through its dynamic sense of the multicultural, 'London taught other cities how to become metropolises'. How, though, does an urban mix, such a natural phenomenon in areas such as Old Compton Street (left), Brick Lane (centre) and Electric Avenue (right), translate into current architectural form? Here Melvin looks at the work of three London-based practices that have all worked on community schemes that engender notions of inclusiveness.

Long before London gave birth to the concept of culture, as the Cambridge art-historian Peter de Bolla recently claimed it did, it was already what we would call multicultural: composed of numerous different communities that existed in some degree of mutual interdependency. The city has always fed on immigrants, from royal spouses and even the occasional prime minister, to street sweepers. This composition was, and is, an essential part of London's character.

De Bolla dates the appearance of culture as the middle of the 18th century, and ascribes its emergence to the particular conditions of London during this period. New money, institutions and social relations, together with the concept of aesthetics, required a move away from the old static model of artistic production between patron and artist, who was now forced to navigate the ebbs and flows of continually fluctuating social and economic conditions. While Vienna and Moscow vied for the title of the third Rome, Constantinople (the second holder of that venerable title) wondered whether it should be glancing at Cordoba, Damascus or Baghdad, Paris mopped up blood and New York had only just recovered from the shock of no longer being New Amsterdam, London was creating the modern novel, hosting premieres of some of Haydn's finest works, and its philharmonic society was

Culture in 18th-century London was quite close to the modern concept of multiculturalism. It was the means by which the new, the fresh and innovative could be brought into some sort of relationship with each other. It did not emerge from Dr Johnson's dining table amid ribs of beef, quarts of claret and dry wit. It evolved from the interweaving of social circumstances and explicitly embraced cosmopolitanism.

Brick Lane, London E1

Brick Lane lies just to the east of the ancient boundary of the City of London, an area traditionally used for activities that were prohibited within the tightly controlled city walls. Here, informal, untaxed commercial activities could take place, relations between master and apprentice were subject to less scrutiny, and religious worship was less restricted. These conditions appealed to immigrant communities, from the Huguenots in the late 17th century, who built a church and the wonderful houses where they plied their skill in weaving, to the Jewish refugees from tsarist pogroms in the late 19th century, to more recent groups, largely from Bangladesh. Although each community has brought its own traditions, all have contributed to the diversity of Brick Lane, and London in general. Below, a new culture signals its presence against the standard terraced houses with almost the flair of a Las Vegas resort.

Electric Avenue, Brixton, London SW9
Sometime in the late 19th century, someone had the idea of creating a relatively upmarket shopping district in the inner London suburb of Brixton, which, well within memory, had been open fields, interspersed with quite large villas inhabited by prosperous professionals and merchants. It never really caught on, but the relics of grandeur remained, even as the area became home to more diverse groups of recent immigrants, from the West Indies, Africa and, even more recently, South America. It established a physical generosity that permitted a certain cultural generosity to take root.

Old Compton Street, London W1
London's Soho always held out the possibility of fleshly pleasures that were hard to obtain in the rest of the city. At a time when British food was a byword for revulsion, and British people were generally considered to be sexually frustrated, Soho had the best (most diverse and least British) restaurants. And prostitution, if not overt, was at least available. Recently this repression has transformed into an open display of tolerance and diversity, as Old Compton Street has become a focus for the gay community, though without excluding other groups.

gearing up to commission that epitome of Kultur, Beethoven's Ninth. At the same time, Britain's wealthiest were filling their town and country houses with paintings the quality and like of which had not been seen in the islands since Cromwell removed Charles I's collection as decisively as the axeman did his head.

Culture in 18th-century London was quite close to the modern concept of multiculturalism. It was the means by which the new, the fresh and innovative could be brought into some sort of relationship with each other. It did not emerge from Dr Johnson's dining table amid ribs of beef, quarts of claret and dry wit. It evolved from the interweaving of social circumstances and explicitly embraced cosmopolitanism. Music from Mitteleurop, concepts from Classicism and sugar from the West Indies were all grist to the same mill, and culture was the net effect. Culture, too, was not necessarily elitist (it was not until the 19th century that it was really to take on two unfortunate connotations: its connection with Nationalism and its implication of elitism). However, it helped to be literate: the serialised tribulations of Samuel Richardson's fictitious heroine Clarissa may add up to the most intimidating novel this side of Henry James and the longest in the English language, but in depicting troubled personal relationships between young adults, it had something of the popular appeal that we might find in *Friends* or *Men Behaving Badly*.

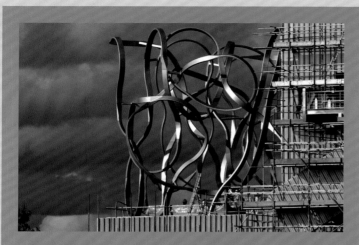

WILL ALSOP ARCHITECTS
Top: Goldsmiths College (University of London), New Cross (2005)
Middle: Queen Mary's College Medical Research Building, Whitechapel (2005)
Bottom: The School of the Future (sketch for DfEE generic project)
Alsop's practice is profoundly influenced by contact with the community his projects serve, but, unlike most so-called community architects, he sees the creative act itself, rather than consultation about 'need' or 'aspiration', as the best vehicle for participation.

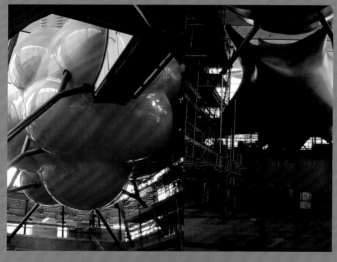

Culture arose at a time when old certainties of hierarchy, relationships and emotional experience were overthrown. It paved the way for the conditions of dynamism, restlessness, the *unheimlich* and sensory overload that Simmel a century ago, and Marshall Berman more recently, associated with modernity. London taught other cities how to become metropolises.

There are new Jerusalems and numbered successions of Athens, Romes and Venices, but London has no seconds, except nominally in Ontario. True, London exported a few architectural set pieces, and replicas of St Martin-in-the-Fields brought solace to many a colonial officer from Accra to Madras, but they were no synecdoche for the whole city. Instead, its inheritance is of processes rather than products, and it bifurcates into two particular bequests. One is culture in the sense of Kultur; the other is multiculturalism. Between the two, and impossible without them, comes 'culcha', the often immigrant-led mechanism by which the mores of the otherwise dispossessed and marginalised are made visible on the streets. Increasingly, since at least the 1950s, culcha has had a bearing on Kultur. It would be a brave architect, artist or writer who would admit to ignoring Punk or *i-D* magazine. And for architects at least, government diktats increasingly demand that buildings permit 'access' by controlling sources of funding for public buildings, and through other measures such as the Disability Discrimination Act that stipulates that no-one should be barred from making full use of a public amenity.

Perhaps less than any other medium of cultural production, architecture cannot escape this co-mingled trinity of Kultur, culcha and multiculturalism. But paradoxically the relationship is also deeply ambiguous. Architecture's own limitations are the first element of this ambiguity. The late Katherine Shonfield, one of the most acute commentators on the condition of London before her premature death in September 2003, was responsible for a powerful paper outlining how three locations – Electric Avenue in Brixton, Brick Lane in Spitalfields and Old Compton Street in Soho – had each become beacons of tolerance and cultural mixing, not entirely by accident but certainly not through the conscious intent of their designers or builders. It was social processes that had first infiltrated and later adapted these innocuous pieces of urban fabric. Brixton has a large Afro-Caribbean population, Brick Lane is the heart of London's Bangladeshi community, while Old Compton Street caters to the gay community. What made Shonfield's paper especially apposite was that a lone bomber had targeted these unconsciously evolved locations precisely because they represented ideas of tolerance.

Being able to control and possibly replicate phenomena such as those described by Shonfield would prolong a politician's career as effectively as the philosopher's stone extended life, so it is no surprise that both Blair's national government and Mayor Ken Livingstone's policies explicitly try to promote 'inclusiveness'. The problem is not so much the aim as the means. As Richard Sennett pointed out recently, people perceive their surroundings as a series of fragments rather than the grand, overarching whole so beloved by politicians and architects. But these fragments are extraordinarily difficult to represent. A map of London's ethnicity depicts the predominant groups in particular areas as amorphous splodges – almost as if appropriating the colour-coding of Patrick Abercrombie's plan for postwar reconstruction that showed areas according to predominant activity. Just as Abercrombie's means of representation enshrined the disastrous policy of 'zoning', so adopting his technique to show another phenomenon that benefits from interactivity is far from ideal. Above all, by concentrating on what can be defined, it overlooks what can't be, such as the locations that Shonfield identified.

The answer promoted by today's politicians is 'consultation'. John Jenner, whose firm Greenhill Jenner

local fears that one community was encroaching on the amenities of another came to the fore in a way that no Abercrombie-esque planning diktat would ever have identified. Consultation helps to define the brief, but does not in itself generate architecture. Greenhill Jenner's community centre is skilfully designed to accommodate the unfamiliar mix of services that such centres are encouraged to include, with two attractive pyramidal-roofed multifunction rooms, but with little obvious trace of the problems noted during the consultation.

Jenner's project is not much more than a stone's throw from Will Alsop's Fawood Children's Centre (⌂ Vol 75, No 3, May/June, 2004, pp 101–5), which shows a rather different approach to consultation. For Alsop, consultation has to infuse the entire design process encouraging, as he puts it, building users to lose

BURRELL FOLEY FISCHER
Angell Town estate, Brixton (1992–3)
The practice combines, and draws mutual benefit from, expertise in cultural buildings such as cinemas and theatres, and urban regeneration projects, especially in housing. It was one of five architects selected to rebuild the Angell Town estate in Brixton, one of London's most ethnically diverse regions, but where the residents effectively galvanised themselves to form effective and informed client bodies. The result was to draw the best out of their architects, and to produce high-quality and attractive housing that deliberately reflects London's housing typology, but also provides flexible accommodation for people who may never have the means to move, and whose needs are not necessarily standard.

works extensively on projects in challenging locations that depend on cocktails of public funds, explains that whether finance comes directly from public coffers, or indirectly through the National Lottery (the distributors of which are bound by government guidelines), consultation is absolutely essential. Consultation is necessarily an open-ended process with unpredictable outcomes, but it can have benefits.

Jenner lists the steps in the process, liaising with steering groups and open meetings, with bewildering fluency. He cites a community centre in Brent, a deprived part of northwest London with a diverse ethnic mix. The new centre replaces a collection of prefabricated huts and adjoins a recreation ground. Across the ground a redundant school has been re-established as a private Hindu foundation school, and is itself just across the road from London's most famous Hindu temple. During consultation,

their inhibitions with a drink and express their ideas with a paint brush. The idea is to treat the world as a kind of extended art school where the aim is to devolve creative control over the immediate environment to local communities.

There is a striking similarity between Alsop's projects designed 'in consultation' and those designed without. All share an exuberance of form and colour, and convey a zest and *joie de vivre* that 'social architecture' often lacks. Whether this is really tapping into a deep vein of 'creativity' lying latent in all communities, or whether it is simply an extension of Alsop's own personality, is a moot point, but perhaps not the main issue. The simple act of participating in a part of the design process embeds the participants more deeply in a design than if it were just handed down, and this invitation to play (in the Huizingarian sense) weaves an important aspect of human experience into them. Also, the message that social projects need not be po-faced should not be lost on architects.

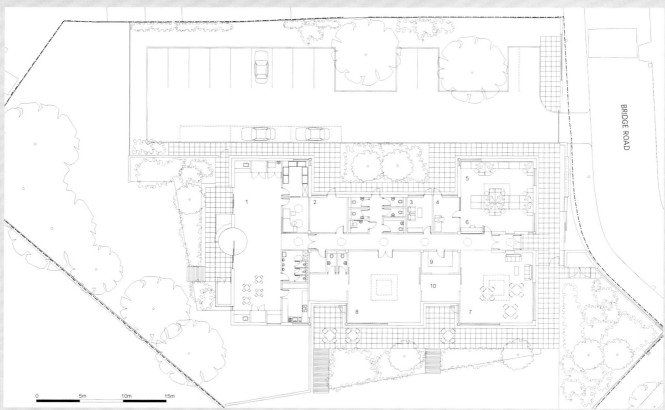

BRIDGE ROAD

0   5m   10m   15m

GREENHILL JENNER ARCHITECTS
Top right and left: Queen's Road Community Centre, Waltham Forest (2002–)
Plan and bottom image: Sure Start Central Brent (2005)
These two community centres by Greenhill Jenner, both in deprived areas of London, were built with help from central government to provide facilities intended to consolidate families and communities. They combine crèches with training facilities for new parents and family support services. Queen's Road also offers lifelong learning, while the Brent centre, with its two top-lit, multipurpose spaces, can accommodate sport and youth activities.

John Burrell, whose firm Burrell Foley Fischer has worked in Brick Lane and Brixton, warns against the danger of loading too much expectation onto architecture. Many of the problems are at root social issues, and architecture's contribution to solving them is limited. He hinges a specific diagnosis around the concept of choice to which every politician has to pay lip service. Affluence gives the bourgeoisie the choice of where to live and how to educate their children. But the poor can only enjoy choice if it is incorporated into the design process. In the jargon, 'consultation' leads to 'empowerment'. This sounds eminently reasonable, and it might allow a very wide degree of choice, but it only happens at one point of the process – a little like the Islamic fundamentalist concept of democracy where everyone has one vote, once, but as soon as it is made that choice is fixed. It suits politicians because they can be seen to be offering 'choice'. However, that choice is not a blank cheque. Only increased affluence brings any further choice beyond that inbuilt within the design.

Typically, basic market-sale apartments are smaller and lower in specification than anything the affordable sector builds. But no-one moves into them with the expectation of staying more than a few years; rising up the salary scale, or perhaps moving in with a partner and pooling incomes, increases the choice. Traditionally, housing associations and local authorities offered much less mobility, though some of the more far-sighted, such as the Peabody Trust, are offering both more flexible forms of tenure and architecture more closely adapted to particular phases of life.

So consultation is a pre-architectural process, necessary but not sufficient, and its relationship to design is complex and indirect. It may help to establish a brief, but it does not roll out a design. Burrell suggests that consultation with some Asian communities has effect on detail, such as additional doors for each gender to enter or leave the room separately, but these are hardly design generators. Consultation cannot in itself account for the evident similarities in certain types of community projects, in particular the timber finishes and the relationship between inside and out mediated through large windows and devices such as pergolas. Some of these can be attributed to Modernism: its claims to be functional and perhaps its universal aspirations. Other reasons are associative: timber might denote softness rather than evoke the harsh associations of concrete. And the ease of flow between interior and exterior is perhaps more practical than anything else, reflecting the semisocial uses of community centres.

These features may not add up to what the great architectural taxonomist Heinrich Wölfflin would have considered a style, but the multiplicity of their origins does show something of the numerous levels of influence and aspiration that such a project can have. Jenner's colleague Tom Hopes adds: 'People say we have a certain style. I don't know how it relates [to the aims of the project], but I am sure it does.' This is an implicit recognition that there is an undefinable, imaginative challenge that lies beyond analysis of consultation data: for want of a better word, it might be called 'design'.

Both Greenhill Jenner and Burrell Foley Fischer contributed to the reconstruction of the Angell Town estate in Brixton. This was one project where a local community, led by the charismatic Dora Boatemah, managed to take over responsibility for rebuilding an estate from local government or a national government agency. The social composition of the estate is mixed, but its architecture is not a simple analogue of this diversity. What the community wanted as much as decent homes was to feel that their locality was a genuine part of London, and not some isolated ghetto, and by extension to feel as if they were a contiguous part of London's social fabric.

The basic model is the street of terraced houses, perhaps the most characteristic of London's building types, and both firms reworked this idiom into quite sophisticated Modernist compositions, expressing individual volumes and using layers to filter public and private spaces. Intended to last for the whole life of their occupants, the homes illustrate Burrell's point about choice. Their designs have to anticipate possible needs by decades. But the spaces they include for lifts that might need to be installed as residents lose their mobility, in the meantime adds up to a few square metres of extra space. However, in extending the tradition of the terraced house, these buildings are symbolically being absorbed into, and simultaneously modifying, the character of London itself, as have immigrant communities for two thousand years.

Appropriating London's most characteristic building type as a symbol of integration is one sign of the city itself providing the means and stimuli for multicultural activity. This has a nonphysical counterpart in the way certain basic social functions have consistently taken place on the same spot despite changes in the social order. Peter Ackroyd in *London the Biography* describes how a Huguenot church, built in Spitalfields in 1744, became a synagogue in 1898 and a mosque in 1975. What remains constant is the site's spiritual function, absorbing the traditions of each incoming community.

'Architects,' says Burrell, 'can be good at designing cheap, ingenious things.' In other words, giving more from the same resources. But that ingenuity needs to open up possibilities rather than be devised to suit single and precise functions. The greatest force for integration is the intertwined traditions and fabric of the city – both evidence of, and encouraging, integration, as in the subconsciously evolved conditions of places like Old Compton Street, Electric Avenue and Brick Lane, whose totemic tolerance was enough to provoke the horrifying nail-bomb attacks mentioned earlier.

But these locations also offer the reverse. Their dynamism shows the rich dynamic that multiculturalism can generate without any conscious architectural input. The challenge for architects is to combine facets such as Jenner's acute sensitivity, Burrell's ingenuity and Alsop's creativity to take it to another level. ∆

New photography of London was specifically shot for this issue of ∆ by Sue Barr, a photography tutor at the Architectural Association in London. She is also the photographer of *London Caffs*, written by Edwin Heathcote (Wiley-Academy, 2004) and *Barbican: Penthouse Over the City*, written by David Heathcote (Wiley-Academy, 2004). She has just completed the international photography for *The 70s House* in the *Interior Angles* series, written by David Heathcote, to be published in late 2005 by Wiley-Academy.

Queens from above
On the streets and from the air, Queens resembles a crazy quilt patched together with few matching parts in a street plan created by extending the Manhattan grid east and the Brooklyn grid north, superimposing the two with traces of Colonial road and Indian paths and surrounding them all with superhighways.

CRAZY QUILT QUEENS

Spreading out over almost 120 square miles on the northwest corner of Long Island, across the East River from Manhattan, Queens is physically the largest borough in the City of New York, and the second most populous and most ethnically diverse county in the US. Its 2.2 million residents come from 81 different countries, and nearly half are foreign-born. Writer **Jayne Merkel** and photographer **Julian Olivas** describe the architectural diversity of Queens – a combination in which architectural and ethnic characteristics rarely coincide. Most of the borough's residents and institutions occupy structures built by those that came before them. Queens is in almost perpetual flux.

The heart of the upper-middle-class community of Forest Hills is the model railway-suburb of Forest Hills Gardens laid out by Grosvenor Atterbury and Frederick Law Olmsted Jnr in 1911 for the philanthropic Russell Sage Foundation.

Contextual housing
This typical Queens block in Flushing, with modern terraced houses in various styles, coexists with older, traditional single-family houses and high-rise apartments. But it is not just styles and periods that are mixed in the area; so are building types and housing densities.

The Shree Swaminarayan Mandir temple, designed by Stapati Ganapati (1973–7), is set behind a decorative fence on Bowne Street in a residential area of Flushing.

Some early 20th-century single-family housing blocks in Flushing resemble those found in small towns and suburbs throughout the US.

Most visitors to New York land in the Borough of Queens, home to La Guardia and JFK airports. But driving into the city centre, they are more likely to fixate on the distant postcard view of the Manhattan skyline than notice the landscape that surrounds them, as the odd mix of terraced houses, low-rise apartments, industrial buildings, billboards and cemeteries here does not coalesce into an obvious image. It is the picture of diversity itself. However, it is not the kind of diversity that visitors find on the streets if they venture into the various Queens neighbourhoods, where there are signs in Spanish, Chinese, Korean, Italian, Greek, Russian, Tagalog, French and Creole, as well as shop windows filled with saris and warm empanadas for sale, shop fronts turned into open-air markets, men smoking water pipes in coffee shops, and Peking ducks hanging next to roasted pigs.

However, the architecture is less exotic, as most of it was built in the early 20th century when immigrants to New York came mainly from Europe and expressed their aspirations with Anglo-American forms.

Because Queens has more land (half that of the entire city) and was developed later than its neighbouring boroughs, it has been fertile ground for dreamers. Not long after British settlers living under Dutch rule in Manhattan moved to Flushing in 1643, the area became a refuge for religious freedom. The house that the English Quaker leader John Bowne built here in 1661 still stands, as does the 1694 Friends Meeting House, though Hindu and Buddhist temples now occupy nearby streets.

In the 1870s, William Steinway moved his piano factory from Manhattan to Queens (whose forests could provide the required timber), building a town for his workers of brick terraced houses, parks and even a church in the village of Astoria. By 1911, Forest Hills Gardens, the model suburb that the philanthropic Russell Sage Foundation had hired architect Grosvenor Atterbury and landscape architect Frederick Law Olmsted Jnr to create, was taking form around the railway station. Two years later, the Queensboro Corporation began construction of romantic garden apartments in Jackson Heights, the plan for which was based on the city block proposed by architect Andrew J Thomas. Also using the grid as a framework, Henry Wright, Clarence Stein and Frederick Ackerman designed the 'new town' of Sunnyside Gardens (where Lewis Mumford proudly lived) for the City Housing Corporation in 1924. Its modest red-brick town houses and apartments surround 70 verdant acres of long, narrow blocks with gardens in the centre and tight rows of trees on the street.

Although most New York City social housing was built after the Second World War in run-down areas of the Bronx, northern Manhattan and Brooklyn, the largest social-housing project in the country – and one of the best – is in Astoria. The brown-brick Queensbridge Houses, with 3,149 units that are home to more than 7,000 residents in 26 six-storey buildings, were built in 1939. However, along with a number of large social-housing projects on the Rockaway peninsula, they are exceptional in a borough created mostly by private enterprise. Even Voorhees, Walker, Foley & Smith architects' austere flat-roofed housing in the green-belt suburb of Fresh Meadows was built by the New York Life Insurance company. Queens, which has all kinds of apartment buildings as well as some big houses with big gardens, is composed mainly of modest single-family and two-family houses, attached or on small plots, built piecemeal and gradually over time. And since much of the housing stock is at least half a century old, even once-unified blocks now have houses with different rooflines, sidings and entrances.

Bricks and mortar were not the dreamers' only tools. In the days of silent movies, and before the US film industry moved to Hollywood, fantasies were projected on the silver screen at the Astoria Studios (from 1919), so it is somewhat ironic that the film and television industry thriving at Silvercup Studios and the Kaufman Astoria Studios in Queens today is called Hollywood East. Queens was also the home of the New York World's Fairs of 1939 and 1964, which took place in the 1,316-acre Flushing Meadows Park where the old pavilions now house museums and theatres. Even La Guardia Airport, which opened in 1939, was a by-product of the 1939 World's Fair, and of the subways built in the 1930s – its runways are made of landfill dredged from the tunnels.

But a map of Queens suggests a nightmare. The borough is intersected and surrounded by highways, bridges, tunnels and tracks – a tangle that is orderly compared to the street grid. It is an overlay like Peter Eisenman's superimposed grid at the Wexner Center, because the Manhattan grid was extended east into Queens, while the Brooklyn grid grew north creating an overlay with numerous wedges among the blocks, which are also cut through by vestiges of colonial roads and Native American paths. To make things worse, numbered avenues running East to West are intersected by numbered streets, roads and drives.

Long Island City
Nevertheless, Queens is thriving. The Long Island City art district has been growing steadily, if incrementally, since 1971 when museum director Alanna Heiss founded P.S.1, a nonprofit exhibition, performance and studio space for artists in an abandoned public school on Jackson Avenue, between 46th Avenue and 46th Road. The building was renovated by Shael Shapiro in 1976, and then more extensively and dramatically remodelled by Los Angeles architect Frederick Fisher in 1997. Now affiliated with the Museum of Modern Art (MoMA), the lively *Kunsthalle* is the primary venue for emerging artists in New York. It has gradually helped attract artists to underused industrial buildings in the area, though there is little evidence of their presence on the street, except for 5 Pointz, a block-long warehouse across the street that has been converted into artist studios and covered with graffiti-inspired murals.

A mile-and-a-half north, Mark di Suvero and artists with studios nearby created the Socrates Sculpture Park on an overgrown site facing the East River in 1986. Four years earlier, just across the street, the sculptor Isamu Noguchi and architect Shogi Sazao had carved the Noguchi museum out of a 1928 photo-engraving plant. Its facilities were sensitively upgraded by Sage and Coombe Architects last year. The Noguchi museum is one of the few places in

Immigrant interventions using existing buildings
The collage of shop fronts on 94th Street in the Jackson Heights business district reflects the lively mix of populations and commercial additions to the neighbourhood.

Shop fronts on Flushing's main shopping street are stacked three storeys high, their colourful canopies vying for attention by advertising wares in two or more languages.

A corner diner in Flushing, similar to those found throughout the New York and New Jersey suburbs, has been transformed into East Lake Restaurant with its colourful Chinese characters, a carousel-like marquee and dragons guarding the entrance.

Artists' reinterpretations of the urban/suburban
The graffiti covering the 5 Pointz artists' studios in a converted industrial warehouse in Long Island City aestheticises cultural traditions of the ghetto rather than the heritage of most of the artists who work there.

Queens where the ethnicity of the builders is evident in the architecture. Though Noguchi was just half-Japanese, being born in Los Angeles and living in Japan only as a boy, the sensibility of his father's native land is evident in his spare, subtle, nature-oriented work and in the building created to house it.

Several miles east, MoMA acquired the old Swingline Staples factory in 1999 for storage, then decided to hold exhibitions there while its mid-Manhattan building was under construction (2002–04). And people came. Los Angeles architect Michael Maltzen designed the temporary galleries in what became known as MoMA QNS, and Cooper, Robertson & Partners created the overall plan, permanent storage and study space.

Several other nonprofit art spaces have since emerged between the two MoMA outposts. The most architecturally interesting is Maya Lin's 2002 conversion of a 1908 tram-repair shop for the Sculpture Center gallery, which manages to look untouched despite being opened up and filled with light. However, although there is subway service, because the galleries here are not within easy walking distance of one another this growing art district is neither as visible nor as cohesive as that in Manhattan. Still, the Dorsky Gallery found that artists began dropping by once the gallery moved from SoHo into a crisp, remodelled, light-filled, mixed-use building that shares a block with distinctly unrenovated spaces housing a jewellery workshop, other industrial enterprises, old apartment buildings, a Philippine corner grocery and the tiny offices of *Prometheus International*, the largest Bangla weekly outside Bangladesh. The strange streetfellows face a square filled with a park, where cricket matches are played alongside basketball and baseball. On the east side of the park, a Korean Seventh Day Adventist church inhabits an old, vaguely classical structure, and Iglesia S Cristo has a vaguely Gothic one; both were obviously built for earlier congregations. The neighbourhood also includes an old Italian restaurant and a new Latin American one – La Vuela – which holds art shows and has live music.

The only real anomaly is the stepped-back, green-glass-walled, 48-storey Citicorp Tower built by Skidmore, Owings & Merrill in 1989, at a time when a commercial district was expected to evolve. Four years earlier, developers of the International Design Center of New York had acquired a group of abandoned factories and converted them, according to a master plan by IM Pei & Partners, with Gwathmey Siegel as architects, to furniture and fabric showrooms. Alas, though artists and their followers were willing to trudge out to Long Island City, decorators and architects were

not. All that is left of the pipe dream are the big red letters IDCNY on the roof. The cavernous buildings now house offices of the New York City Department of Design and Construction, School Construction Authority and Department of Transportation. Though the bare, light-filled postindustrial spaces inside have been stripped of all cultural connotations because of the city's multicultural work force, lunch tables in the big atrium spaces surrounded by open offices offer sights and smells that it would be surprising to find even at the UN.

Now, with the help of the Empire State Development Corporation, private developers are attempting to create a new Manhattan-style residential community on a formerly industrial, 72-acre riverside site in Hunter's Point, a stable, old-fashioned neighbourhood of terraced houses, apartments above retail premises, six-storey walk-ups (tower blocks without lifts) and small commercial buildings. Queens West already has several waterside parks, a residential tower by Cesar Pelli and apartments by Perkins Eastman. The Rockrose Corporation is also building a cluster of largely residential blocks designed by Arquitectonica on the 20 acres where the Pepsi-Cola bottling works used to be. The plan was to have a series of gridded facades that would read from Manhattan as clearly as the old Pepsi sign that remains as a landmark. But recently, crystalline towers have also been envisioned. If New York had won the bid for the 2012 Olympics, the south end of the Queens West parcel would have become the site of an Olympic village designed by Thom Mayne's Morphosis.

Just north of here, the Silvercup Studios, founded in 1983 in the landmark Silvercup Bakery, gradually developed a

Sage and Coombe Architects, Isamu Noguchi Foundation and Garden Museum, Long Island City, 2004
The Japanese-American sculptor Isamu Noguchi first moved his home and studio across the East River from Manhattan to an industrial site on Long Island City in Queens in 1961. Once established there, he designed a garden of his own around the converted factory buildings. In 1985, the studios and garden were opened to the public as the Isamu Noguchi Foundation and Garden Museum. Offering a haven from the city and an opportunity to view a comprehensive collection of Noguchi's sculptures, the facilities were sympathetically refurbished by Sage and Coombe Architects in 2004.

series of sound stages, video production studios and rooftop shooting spaces with Manhattan skyline views. In 2004, the studios announced plans to build a 2-million-square-foot mixed-use development with the Richard Rogers Partnership and NBBJ Architecture on an adjacent six-and-a-half-acre site. The development will have a public waterfront esplanade, apartments and shops as well as studios.

Not far away, the New York developer William Kaufman has transformed the historic Astoria Studios into block after block of modern production facilities that are now known as the Kaufman Astoria Studios. And the nonprofit Museum of the Moving Image, designed by Gwathmey Siegel, is here, too.

The only word to describe these places, where people come from everywhere and produce programmes seen all over the world, is international. The rest of Queens is multicultural – a very different thing, more like a stew than a blended broth.

Steps away from the Kaufman Astoria Studios, on Steinway Street, are Colombian restaurants and banks, bakeries, party shops and clothing shops catering to various ethnicities. Next come Middle Eastern coffee shops and grocers, though only the beautiful Mombar Egyptian Restaurant makes an architectural statement, its facade embedded with coloured tiles in abstract shapes. Down side streets, Brazilian flags fly on household porches. Most professional offices, however, carry Greek names. Greek families moved to Astoria in the early 20th century as the domed 1927 Saint Demetrios Greek Orthodox cathedral attests, but after immigration restrictions were lifted in 1965, Astoria became the largest Greek community outside

Greece. Now there are the headquarters of the many Greek-owned furniture stores and coffee shops throughout the area, and numerous lively Greek restaurants with pavements that turn into dance halls on summer evenings. But this is not reflected in the architecture here, except in the jewel-like 1980 Greek Orthodox Sacred Patriarchal Monastery of Saint Irene on the Ecumenical Patriarchs' Way (23rd Avenue) between 36th and 37th streets, which is flanked by town houses decorated with a Mediterranean air.

Jackson Heights, Forest Hills, Flushing
The liveliest ethnic mix is in Jackson Heights, where Colombian, Peruvian and Argentinean restaurants, Ethel's Design Boutique from Rio, an Ecuadorian steak house and Music-Mex cluster together on Roosevelt Avenue near Zapateria Mexico, which sells cowboy boots, Tejano hats and sombreros. Women walk by wearing saris, bought around the corner on 74th Street, where the Burala Emporium sells books in Urdu, Hindi, Punjabi, Bengali and English, the Apna Bazaar sells South Asian herbs, and Karat 22 specialises in enormous filigreed gold Indian necklaces – all of these exotic items displayed in typical American aluminium-framed shop fronts. The popular Jackson Diner Indian restaurant recently installed 1950s American 'googie' decor (the lively style made popular by LA coffee shops in the 1950s), but the sounds of the sitar echo from record stores, and the Eagle Movie Theater shows Bollywood films.

In the nearby Jackson Heights historic district (between 78th and 88th streets), the names of the Romanesque revival 'Towers Apartments', Mansard-roofed 'Chateau', 'Laurel Court', 'Fillmore Hall', 'Spanish Gardens' and 'English Convertible Country Homes' suggest that their developers were trying to attract tenants with both British and continental aspirations. The buildings were initially 'restricted' (barring Jews, Catholics and blacks), but soon Jewish-, Italian- and Irish-Americans moved in, and the neighbourhood is now one of the most diverse in the world.

Anglophilia was rampant in the US in the early 20th century, when immigrants tried to assimilate as quickly as possible. Where Colonial houses were not in vogue, Tudor ones were. Forest Hills Gardens, built on 142 acres by philanthropist Margaret Olivia Slocum Sage, a devotee of Ebenezer Howard's Garden Cities movement, is a model of modern suburban planning, with

Modern architecture
Polshek Partnership, Flushing Regional Branch Library, 1998
The library is both literally and symbolically a beacon of light in the community.

Peter Muller Munk, Unisphere, Queens Theatre-in-the-Park, Flushing Meadows Park, 1964
The Unisphere, created for the New York World's Fair with landscape architect Gilmre Clark, is still the centrepiece of Flushing Meadows Park, which is home to the Queens Theatre-in-the-Park.

Greg Lynn, Michael McInturf and Doug Garafalo, New York Presbyterian (Korean) Church, Sunnyside, 1996–9
The 'Korean Church', as it is commonly known, was built on top of the Art Deco Knickerbocker Laundry. Though it provides striking views of Manhattan, its computer-generated design pays little heed to the character of the Sunnyside neighbourhood.

terraced houses, apartments, an inn and a shopping district clustered near the railway station, 1,500 single-family houses with lawns, and a system of parks beyond. Designed to resemble an English village, it even has a private tennis club (like that at Wimbledon) where the us Open was played until the US Tennis Center was built in nearby Flushing Meadows Park in 1978. The apartments were intended for local workers, but quickly attracted the upper middle classes, and though oriented to the Long Island Railroad, Forest Hills is now served by four subway lines. The 'town' is so attractive that it inspired the adjacent planned communities of Rego Park and Kew Gardens, and is now surrounded by modern mid-rise and high-rise apartments in the larger community of Forest Hills. Like Jackson Heights, it started out Protestant, later became predominantly Jewish, attracted second- and third-generation Italians, and now has many Russian residents, too. But Forest Hills, unlike most of Queens, remains predominantly white.

Jamaica, on the other hand, is thought to be largely black, since it has many African, African-American and African-Caribbean residents (from Jamaica, Haiti, Trinidad and Tobago), as well as historically black residential areas; for example, swanky St Albans, where jazz greats Count Basie, Billie Holiday and Ella Fitzgerald all once lived. But a recent survey showed that in fact it is the most racially diverse neighbourhood in Queens, as it also has newcomers from Puerto Rico, the Dominican Republic, Russia, India, Pakistan, Bangladesh, China, the Philippines and even Alaska, as well as a number of older Jewish and Irish residents who did not follow others to the suburbs. A trading centre where Long Island farmers sold their produce in the 18th century, Jamaica became a retail hub with the arrival of department stores with the subway in the 1930s, but shopping centres built in nearby suburbs in the 1950s led to its decline. Recently, however, downtown Jamaica has become a national outlet for bargain-priced hip-hop fashions sold at Cookies Department Store and many other small shops. In nearby Jamaica Center, where the chain stores are, there is also an interesting Farmers Market with a clerestoried steel portico designed by James McCuller (1997) that recalls the town's origins while adding dining and office space. Jamaica is now the home of the AirTrain to JFK Airport, so another chapter may soon be added to its history.

Many Asian businesspeople arriving at JFK head directly to Flushing, avoiding Manhattan entirely. Although the area was settled by the Dutch and English in the 17th century, and has had black residents since the English Quakers began having slaves, more than a decade ago there were about 110,000 Koreans, 100,000 Northern (Mandarin-speaking) Chinese from Taiwan and 94,000 Indians resident in Flushing. Today, however, many of the Koreans who arrived after immigration quotas were lifted in 1964 have moved to the suburbs, and many more Chinese have arrived. The 14-storey Sheraton Hotel, built by a Chinese businessman, may look American on the outside, sheathed in brick and with pink reflective glass windows, but inside it is a diminutive version of a modern Chinese hotel with a central atrium surrounded by shops.

The colourful glass-walled, block-long, three-storey Flushing Mall across the street, with its open stalls and Chinese wares, brings China to Queens more convincingly. Little English is spoken here. The commercial centre of Flushing along Main Street, Roosevelt Avenue, and Northern and Kissena boulevards pulsates with the energy of a big Asian city. Some 800 restaurants and 35 banks, and Chinese and Korean shops, are interspersed with American chains like Gap, yet the crowds on the streets, the lively window displays and wide-open doors give this place a completely distinctive character.

Down side streets are typical American houses, many occupied by several thrifty Asian families or by one with tenants. Only blocks south of the 17th-century John Bowne House on Bowne Street, amid a cluster of shingle-style, Colonial revival and Prairie-style houses on Ash Street, is the severe, flat-roofed, emphatically horizontal Nichiren Shoshu Temple, designed by Ashikara Associates in 1984 for a congregation that practises a 13th-century type of Japanese Buddhism. A few blocks away is the Postmodern, stucco Won Korean Buddhist Temple, by Bo Yoon & Associates, which was built in 1986. And on Bowne Street itself is Baryn Basu Associates' ornate, stepped Hindu Temple Society of North America (1977). Compared to

these, Greg Lynn, Michael McInturf and Doug Garafalo's folded and pleated 'Korean Church' (officially the New York Presbyterian Church) in Sunnyside, which was built on top of an Art Deco laundry, does not seem strange at all. But, unlike the architects of the Flushing temples who strove to express the traditions of the congregations that built them, the driving force here was neither the culture of the owners nor the Art Deco architecture of the 1932 Knickerbocker Laundry that forms its base, but the way the computer was used in the design process, both to generate forms and link the architects, all of whom lived in different cities. As a result, there is a disconnection from both the physical context and the culture of the congregation. The small Korean scrolls hanging on the walls during the 1999 opening seemed almost intrusive in the vacuous spaces.

Although it, too, is composed of abstract forms and modern materials, the Polshek Partnership's 1998 Flushing Regional Branch Library defines its site and enhances the activity it was built to house. Its shiny blue-glass facade curves along Kissena Boulevard at Main Street, welcoming patrons while reinforcing the street plan. The light-filled spaces inside are always full of readers. Patronage is so brisk that the library is open on Sundays. It is in many ways the symbol and the centre of a community that uses knowledge and hard work to succeed in America.

Polshek also redesigned one of the centrepieces of Flushing Meadows Park. His addition to the New York Hall of Science, completed last year, consists of a sweeping, horizontal, transparent block of new exhibition spaces that complement Harrison & Abramovitz's iconic multicurved Great Hall from the 1964 World's Fair, a soaring cellular concrete structure infilled with cobalt-coloured cast-glass panes. Now, Caples Jefferson Architects is adding a small curving cabaret and a spiralling, oval, 250-seat reception centre for the Queens Theatre-in-the-Park, which was created in 1991 within the cylindrical Theaterama that Philip Johnson built as the New York State Pavilion for the 1964 fair. The addition was inspired by the geometry of the original cylinder and saucers that hover above it on stilts. The domed glass reception centre, punctuated by skylights, will provide a dramatic entrée to the world of the performance and to views of the phantasmagoric remains of old World's Fair dreams.

But not all dreams come true in Queens. Plans for a dramatic multicurved addition to the Queens Museum of Art by Eric Moss were recently cancelled due to disagreements between the architect, city officials and the museum staff, though the scheme had been selected in a well-publicised competition and planning had proceeded for two years. Queens just may be a place that does its best building incrementally, subtly, even surreptitiously as its many layers of society change continually, with surprisingly little friction. The energy on the streets is palpable. The mood upbeat and fleeting. These are difficult phenomena to translate into architectural terms. ⚙

Caples Jefferson Architects, Design for Queens Theatre-in-the-Park extension, 2002–
Caples Jefferson's design for the extension of the Queens Theatre-in-the-Park inserts a spiralling reception area into Philip Johnson's New York State Pavilion building for the 1964 World's Fair.

New photography of Queens was specifically shot for this issue by New York-based photographer Julian Olivas. An architect and helicopter pilot as well as photographer, Olivas heads Global Air-to-Ground, where he combines his three-pronged interests, shooting and flying for architects, builders, universities and corporations. His photographs of buildings, cityscapes, landscapes and people at work have been widely exhibited and received numerous awards. His work can be seen at www.globalairtoground.com.

Rem Koolhaas, McCormick Tribune Campus Center, Illinois Institute of Technology (IIT), Chicago, 2003
The fritted-glass dividing wall between the resource centre and the dining room is illuminated by slot-mounted accent lights. During the day the wall appears transparent. The division of the two spaces is heightened at night as the frit is grazed with light becoming opaque.

FABRICATING PLURALISM

One summer during college, I had a job collecting data on houses that were being reassessed for tax purposes. In the rolling bluegrass of Anchorage, Kentucky, near America's finest horse farms, I would ride my bike through an *allée* of old oak trees to one of those Civil War-era estates that could not be seen from the road. Waiting in the front hall for someone who did not want to answer my questions didn't bother me. I was curious to look inside, and even more so to see what remained of the former slave quarters out back (some were renovated into children's playhouses). Yet, what is unforgettable about these living quarters is the upholstery and oriental rugs. Many of them were worn threadbare in places, and draping the windows were linen and brocade so sun-damaged that light was leaking through them.

No fabric had been allowed to fray in the aspiring middle-class dwellings of my youth. Here, in some of America's old-wealth homes, the surfaces were worn and faded. And to my surprise, there was something relaxed, almost sleepy, about these interiors that exuded a patina of confidence that, I imagine, could only accrue after generations of financial and social comfort.

Rooms of faded fabric are now readily available in a palette known as 'shabby chic'. Colours with names like 'Thoroughbred' appear under the brand that Ralph Lauren

naturally superior and those whose labour they depend upon appear to be naturally inferior. Barthes handed generations of graduate students the conceptual tools for challenging cultural authority by a process of returning that which appears 'natural' to the dynamic history of its making.

Designing a line of clothing, furnishings and fabrics for what might be considered heritage-repair and replacement, lifestyle-industry designers like Ralph Lauren and Martha Stewart do not need to challenge the status quo to profit from the desire to manipulate it. With a full line of tools and techniques, as well as services for faux finishes like 'antiquing' one's books, Martha Stewart leaves no doubt that transforming flea-market purchases into something that could pass as inherited wealth is hard labour (refinishing is never metaphysical), while Polo portrays consumers in the sporting life.

The message is: everything you desire can be purchased, and everything that you buy will appear to have always been part of your life. Designed to resonate with the authority and security of old money, these products come into existence because of the anxiety that drives retail, fashion and cultural assimilation. Polo succeeds because it plays with culture and with the cultural contradictions that riddle social change.

Architects, too, play with culture and cultural contradictions, and use built structures and spaces to deflect and engage dynamic

In an age when culture has become a lifestyle accoutrement, Jamie Horwitz contemplates both the potency and highly transmittable nature of culture. She puts her ideas to the test by looking at the newly completed facilities of some of the greatest places of cultural acquisition in the US – institutes of learning. How might it be possible for university campuses to foster architectural expression that engenders global social exchange while avoiding all the pitfalls of anonymity most commonly associated with the airport lounge?

initiated in 1967 with a collection of men's ties and a story about an American lifestyle that is anti-fashion, like the timelessness of the sporting English aristocracy. Another child of immigrants, Ralph Lauren was born Ralph Lipshitz into a working-class Jewish neighbourhood in the Bronx and, without a formal education in design, he grasped and capitalised on the process of assimilation that sociologists have been trying to theorise for several decades. The intercultural adaptation among social groups striving to assimilate into the economic mainstream is sustained by a form of metaphysics some call the 'metaphysics of Britishness'.[1]

Interpreting the Polo brand as a 'lifestyle' industry, Lauren has succeeded with a line of coordinated paints, wallpapers, rugs, bedding, linens, furniture, accessories, clothing, china, shoes, window frames and treatments, and in turn has become one of the world's richest designers. His success suggests another story as well.

Reducing one strain of old European elegance to a product line, Polo reminds us that culture is not only a noun, but also a verb. As Roland Barthes explains in his essay 'Myth Today', cultural authority is constructed, not natural.[2] The status quo is sustained through a process he calls 'mythification' in which those in power appear to be

social conditions. In this essay, however, I return to something closer to the surface, if not exactly frayed silk and threadbare oriental rugs. By selecting certain materials and finishes, designers intensify the social comforts that do or do not accompany the shape and structure of built form. Colour and light, hard and soft surfaces, as well as the spatial distance and visual connection between circulation and settings, all set the stage and the tone of shared spaces, making them more or less friendly, especially to newcomers.

This is the case on many campuses today, where public and private colleges, universities and research centres are occupied by students, scientists, engineers and others from a broad mix of ethnic backgrounds. And it is increasingly part of the mission of these institutions to engender a social environment that explicitly fosters unbiased exchange. The demands of a programme such as a student centre (one focus of the massive contemporary building campaigns on US campuses) include everything from mailboxes and snack bars, recreational lounges, computer and study centres to dining and meeting rooms. The design challenge in the multicultural traffic flow of higher education is to find an architectural expression that goes beyond the formal language of the air terminal – a model in which the reality of global exchange has generated the uniquely abstract spatial condition of contemporary life.

Jamie Horwitz, *Not my Grandmother's Living Room*
This montage, by the author, edits dreaming girls (the figures are from a painting by Balthus) into the deeply cushioned furnishings of the living room of a fractured and unsettling image of what might be an English country house.

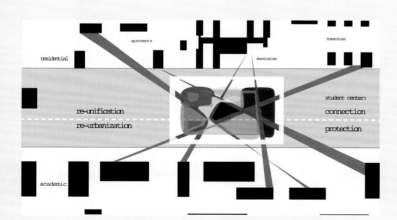

Rem Koolhaas, McCormick Tribune Campus Center, IIT, Chicago, 2003
At the physical heart of the IIT campus, Rem Koolhaas's design captures the 'sum of the student flows, the web of lines that already connect the eastern and western campus destinations' organising and differentiating the activities into a 'dense mosaic' of 'streets, plazas and urban islands'. Two of OMA's circulation diagrams are superimposed here by the author.

Universities, like airport terminals, are powerful nodes in our dispersed, networked and increasingly global market economy. Although different building types, an unexpected mix of the fluid and un-clubby air terminal, and the patterned rituals of a college campus are fashioned together by Rem Koolhaas's design for the McCormick Tribune Campus Center at IIT that opened in 2004. Lines from pedestrian movement, the flows of people passing each other towards their different destinations on campus, form the painterly circulation diagram by Koolhaas's firm OMA.

Unlike any airport, however, the IIT Campus Center in Chicago is also a vibrant hub for students, staff and faculty. This $48-million single-storey rectangle wrapped in glass walls is the size of a city block and is surmounted by a 530-foot-long concrete tube clad in corrugated steel.

By reclaiming a derelict space at the edge of the campus, directly under Chicago's elevated train, Dutch architect Rem Koolhaas applies what he inspired generations of design students to consider in his 1978 book *Delirious New York*: mend the city by incorporating the infrastructure and beauty of its congestion.[3] OMA encased the 'L' in a sound-attenuating material, combining the auditory 'whoosh' of the Chicago Transit Authority trains with the aesthetic buzz of the brilliant lighting design by Melanie Taylor of NBBJ of Seattle.

During an espresso break, or an Internet log-in at the red Broadband Lounge, or during a meal in the restaurant for faculty and guests surrounded by floor-to-ceiling

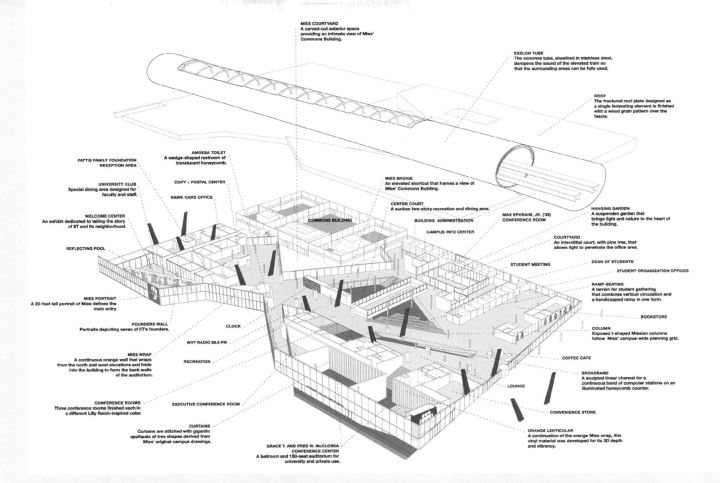

MIES COURTYARD
A carved-out exterior space providing an intimate view of Mies' Commons Building.

EXELON TUBE
The concrete tube, sheathed in stainless steel, dampens the sound of the elevated train so that the surrounding areas can be fully used.

ROOF
The fractured roof plate designed as a single federating element is finished with a wood grain pattern over the fascia.

PATTIS FAMILY FOUNDATION
RECEPTION AREA

AMOEBA TOILET
A wedge-shaped restroom of translucent honeycomb.

UNIVERSITY CLUB
Special dining area designed for faculty and staff.

COPY + POSTAL CENTER

HAWK CARD OFFICE

MIES BRIDGE
An elevated shortcut that frames a view of Mies' Commons Building.

WELCOME CENTER
An exhibit dedicated to telling the story of IIT and its neighborhood.

CENTER COURT
A sunken two-story recreation and dining area.

COMMONS BUILDING

BUILDING ADMINISTRATION

MAX EPHRAIM, JR. ('39)
CONFERENCE ROOM

HANGING GARDEN
A suspended garden that brings light and nature to the heart of the building.

CAMPUS INFO CENTER

REFLECTING POOL

COURTYARD
An interstitial court, with pine tree, that allows light to penetrate the office area.

STUDENT MEETING

DEAN OF STUDENTS

STUDENT ORGANIZATION OFFICES

MIES PORTRAIT
A 20-foot tall portrait of Mies defines the main entry.

RAMP-SEATING
A terrain for student gathering that combines vertical circulation and a handicapped ramp in one form.

FOUNDERS WALL
Portraits depicting seven of IIT's founders.

CLOCK

BOOKSTORE

WIIT RADIO 88.9 FM

COLUMN
Exposed I-shaped Miesian columns follow Mies' campus-wide planning grid.

MIES WRAP
A continuous orange wall that wraps from the north and west elevations and folds into the building to form the back walls of the auditorium.

RECREATION

COFFEE CAFE

BROADBAND
A sculpted linear channel for a continuous band of computer stations on an illuminated honeycomb counter.

LOUNGE

CONFERENCE ROOMS
Three conference rooms finished each in a different Lilly Reich-inspired color.

EXECUTIVE CONFERENCE ROOM

CONVENIENCE STORE

CURTAINS
Curtains are stitched with gigantic appliqués of tree shapes derived from Mies' original campus drawings.

ORANGE LENTICULAR
A continuation of the orange Mies wrap, this vinyl material was developed for its 3D depth and vibrancy.

GRACE T. AND FRED W. McCLOSKA
CONFERENCE CENTER
A ballroom and 150-seat auditorium for university and private use.

etched-glass panels, one floats serenely in the IIT campus centre. By threading traffic through architecture, and urban infrastructure through cultural heritage, its designers play context and circumstance against place and tradition – only partially controlling the complex ambient environment of this urban campus. Instead, the building becomes a vital node in the social and spatial circulation of people, ideas and food, arguably three of the most important elements for introducing and maintaining any kind of cultural pluralism.

Contrast this with the recently constructed pedestrian tunnel at the Detroit International Airport Terminal (2002) that sports a tunnel passage designed by SmithGroup that trumps the former champion of airport walkways, the United Terminal link at Chicago's O'Hare, by bathing hurried travellers in a changing sea of coloured light.

The tunnel is a supremely efficient and visually beautiful people mover, and little else. It connects flights, not people. While the comparison between airport terminals and student centres is limited, it remains pragmatic in the ways that the former create a pedestrian zone for everyone and no-one in particular. They are intentionally asocial, and sociofugal, as well as increasingly elegant and grand.

On the other hand, the University of California San Diego (UCSD) commissioned an exterior walkway of nearly the same size and shape as an airport concourse that offers an object lesson, of sorts, in design criteria for a pluralist society. Following a 1989 campus master-plan by Skidmore Owings & Merrill (SOM), the landscape architect firm of Peter Walker (now Peter Walker Partners) conceived Library Walk not merely as an avenue, but as a structuring and unifying element within the broader circulation network of the campus. Library Walk demonstrates the social power of a wide, straight walkway that gives a clear spatial hierarchy to the campus without imposing a centre.

Rem Koolhaas, McCormick Tribune Campus Center, IIT, Chicago, 2003
By threading the programme throughout the interior circulation paths and ramps, and organising the commercial elements along the street edge of the building, providing convenient access for the neighbourhood, the IIT campus centre both contains and engages an urban condition. 'The main federating element is the roof,' says OMA, 'a continuous concrete slab that shields the campus centre against the noise of the elevated while unifying the heterogeneity below.'

The red Broadband Lounge is lit with simple fluorescent strips mounted to the wall under the white translucent countertop. The glowing counter and glossy red walls create a sophisticated and calm oasis in the busy campus centre.

SmithGroup, Edward H McNamara Terminal/Northwest WorldGateway, Detroit Metropolitan Airport, 2002
A delightful feature of the terminal is a below-ground moving sidewalk in which 264 curved, 14-foot-high art-glass panels, designed by artist Laurel Clark-Fyfe, line the walls of the tunnel.

Peter Walker Partners, Library Walk, University of California San Diego (UCSD), 1994
The concourse-sized walkway gives spatial hierarchy and orientation to the campus while reinventing the student 'centre' as a linear park.

The oversized width of the conduit identifies it as an orientation device (from all the small paths that cross it) and permits multiple lanes of traffic, in both directions. This physical breadth allows cyclists to pass slow walkers without destabilising them, and still leaves room for a group of friends to promenade. The textured and striped paving surface is lined by raised concrete bed-like benches that are large enough for sunbathing or sharing a picnic with a study group.

Each bench houses luminaires that spread their glow close to the ground. These lanterns are a source of continuous low-level lighting – the safest form of street lighting – creating unbroken illumination without the shadows (and hiding places) that surround intense overhead street lights. A continuously lit ground plane also reassures an ageing eye or a person with low vision who cannot quickly adapt to shifts from light to dark.

Architects and landscape architects have much to contribute to the success of organisations and institutions in which working and living with people of similar backgrounds and abilities is less and less the rule. Designers of a 'network society' might also learn from decades of research about communities that define themselves through communication rather than through shared places (or spatial boundaries such as neighbourhood edges). The network theory of social capital derives from the insights of research by Mark S Granovetter. In his influential essay 'The Strength of Weak Ties' (first published in 1973 in the *American Journal of Sociology*), Granovetter traces how 'weak ties', formed by casual acquaintances (outside one's primary circle of co-workers, family or friends), lead to clear advantages; for example, when it comes to something like finding the right

Peter Walker Partners, Library Walk, UCSD, 1994
The Library Walk threads a boardwalk-like space for lingering, reading
or resting on the bed-size concrete benches that house luminaires that
spread a soft continuous light close to the pavement at night.

Goody Clancy Architects, Jean S Yawkey Student Recreation Center, Emmanuel College, Boston, 2004
Perched in the tree tops, the upper lounge has an intimate physical comfort while being visually expansive and open. The sense of warmth is strengthened by the columns' cherry-clad panels and the hemlock-board ceiling that project their glow across the quadrangle in the evening.

A sense of inviting warmth projects out across the Emmanuel College quadrangle from the student centre.

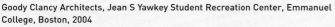

job. Ronald Burt (1992) expanded on this theory, showing that when conversations occur between people from different social networks, even irregular contact can bridge the gaps he refers to as structural holes.[4] Structural holes are a result of being isolated within one's own context, and Burt theorises that value increases by identifying and crossing 'structural holes' in one's organisation or industry, fostering a better understanding of the social structure of competition, or what he calls 'the social capital of structural holes'.

Site and building designs that increase individual and organisational value, rather than primarily drawing attention to themselves, generate settings in which people are invited to 'cross structural holes' that exist among and between social groups, academic disciplines, project teams and personal networks. Among the many new student meeting places across US campuses is one that takes on this particular challenge with considerable skill. Designed by Goody Clancy Architects (Boston) and inaugurated in 2004, the Jean S Yawkey Student Recreation Center at Emmanuel College is nestled into a tight urban campus in Boston, Massachusetts. Like the aforementioned walkway at UCSD, it is also a product of a campus master-plan by the same firm. The building links the residential edge of Emmanuel College through a transparent, 24-foot-high glazed interior passageway to the central campus quadrangle.

Goody Clancy succeeded in having students, faculty and staff engage each other in this central light-filled spine by lining its porous edge with various meeting rooms that encourage circulation back and forth between private and public spaces. This literal transparency extends as well to how the building connects itself to its context, allowing students not only to see themselves, collectively, in the interior space, but also orienting them to the major campus buildings through the large picture window that faces the quadrangle. This new structure dialogues with the older campus buildings, without mirroring them in appearance.

On the mezzanine level the Goody Clancy-designed Emmanuel College recreation centre is a student 'living room' that is wide enough for two rows of clustered furniture, and narrow enough to keep the scale both intimate and visually open. Filled with red and grey leather club-chairs that are deep and soft (some are double-wide), and at the same time upright, the chairs and the space are perfect for relaxing as well as staying alert while reading. Thick carpeting and small tables scattered between columns and wood panels lend a conversational atmosphere, and casters on the chairs make it easy to pull them closer together or further apart, allowing students and faculty to find their comfortable social and spatial distance.

Pluralist societies accrue from economic mobility and social justice. International air terminals, like the railroad stations of the 19th century, give architectural expression to technological advances and capital investment in transportation infrastructure. The architecture of higher education, on the other hand, gives expression to the advances and investment in intellectual capital, and the social exchange and individual momentum through which learning happens.

Campus design is always linked to cultural authority at the same time that it expressly welcomes newcomers and boundary crossers. Being a newcomer is never easy. The longing to blend in is rarely anyone's finest moment. Wonderful designers make use of such contrary sociocultural dynamics to design settings where people who know one another only slightly may detain each other in the expanded spatial threshold of a corridor or a walkway where paths intersect, and where it is possible to linger in visually open settings, comfortable for reading, snacking and talking, as they do in the student centres discussed above. Eventually, as social-cultural patterns change, leaving physical traces of continuous use, these settings may become beautifully faded and worn; this time, if we are lucky, through the fabrication of pluralism. ∆

Goody Clancy set a genial stage for seeing and being seen with the firm's design of the Jean S Yawkey Student Recreation Center at Emmanuel College. The primary staircase links the upper lounge, drawing a prominent figure across the facade and the reflections in the glass rails of the Collegiate Gothic buildings across the quadrangle.

Notes
1 The phrase comes from P Gilroy and H Baker, *There Ain't No Black in the Union Jack: The Cultural Politics of Race and Nation*, University of Chicago Press, 1991. However, it is mentioned widely in contemporary debates about assimilation and multiculturalism in a global economy, for example in: Eric Mark Kramer (ed), *The Emerging Monoculture: Assimilation and the 'Model Minority'*, Praeger Publishers (Westport, CT), 2003.
2 Roland Barthes defined this process in 'Myth Today', which appeared in a 1957 collection of essays entitled *Mythologies*, published by Editions du Seuil, Paris. Selections were translated from the French by Annette Lavers in many English publications. The 13th edition was published by Hill and Wang in 1982.
3 The first publication of Rem Koolhaas's *Delirious New York: A Retroactive Manifesto for Manhattan,* was in 1978. A new edition was published by Monacelli (New York), in 1994.
4 See Ronald S Burt, *Structural Holes: The Social Structure of Competition,* Harvard University Press (Cambridge, MA), 1992.

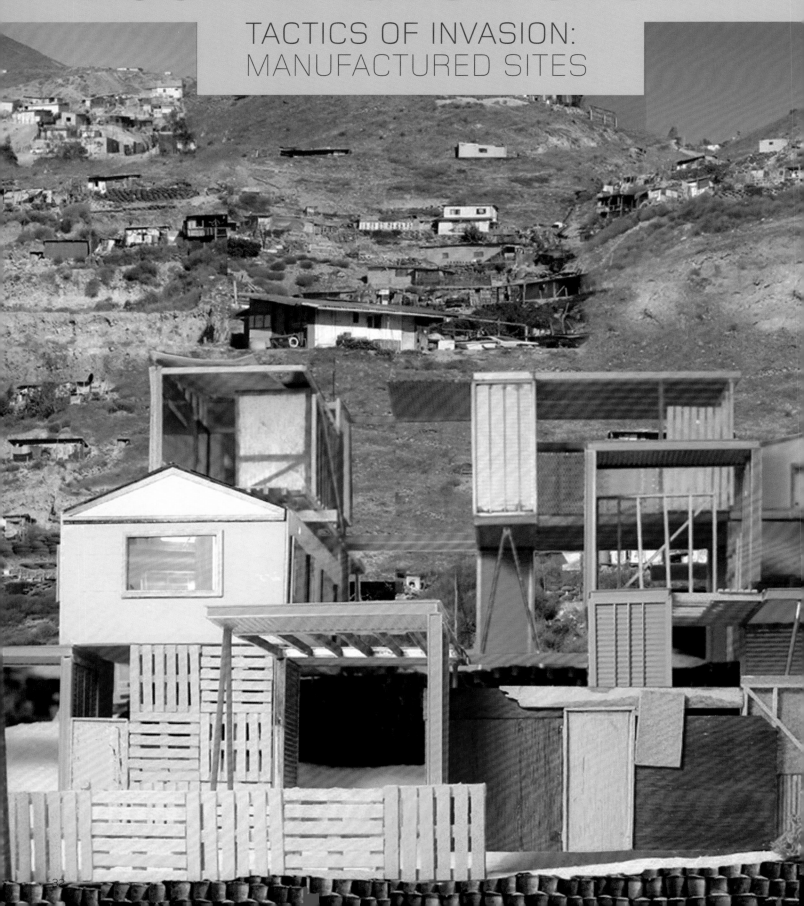

Teddy Cruz describes how his practice in San Diego has used its experience of Mexican/US border conditions to inform a project of 'urban acupuncture' that has the potential to bridge the enormity of a transnational divide that exists between two adjacent communities. In essence a simple prefabricated aluminium frame, Manufactured Sites could provide the much-needed, small-scale infrastructures and services for *favela*-like settlements.

The international border between the US and Mexico at the San Diego/Tijuana checkpoint is the most trafficked in the world. Approximately 60 million people cross annually, moving untold amounts of goods and services back and forth. This contested zone is the site of massive contradiction, defined and redefined every day by the unstable balance of two powerful forces. On one hand are the 'legal' actions and 'official' urban policy prompting the federal government to rethink surveillance infrastructure, incrementally transforming San Diego into the largest gated community, while on the other hand insurgent and 'illegal' actions proliferate in both border cities in smaller-scale, spontaneous occupations and appropriations that seek to blur and transgress the 10-foot-high steel wall that divides these border cities

Even though our practice is primarily interested in challenging the rigidity of San Diego's discriminatory planning regulations and housing policy, it has also been researching, by physically dwelling at the shared edge of these two border cities, the role of housing within the strategies of invasion and appropriation that shape the informal communities of Tijuana. Learning from Tijuana's practices of everyday life has informed our efforts to develop the conceptual tools to rupture the dam that keeps this city from spilling into San Diego. While in San Diego the effort has been to contaminate urban legislature with the 'spillage' of heterogeneity and juxtaposition found in Tijuana, the energies that drive our practice within Tijuana via projects such as Manufactured Sites'have to do with imagining a project of urban acupuncture that can inject services and small infrastructure into the precarious condition of the *favela*-like settlements on the city's periphery.

Manufactured Sites explores the start-up housing processes within Tijuana's slum communities. In his most recent book, *Planet of Slums*,[1] Mike Davis reminds us that one billion people live in slums around the world and that it is in fact in those types of settlements that we can find a laboratory to advance ideas of housing in relation to sustainability, technology and community. Working at the San Diego/Tijuana border allows us to closely observe this phenomenon, as Tijuana's informal periphery is incrementally shaped by nomadic settlements that appear from one day to another, growing at an even faster rate than San Diego's gated communities.

This proximity has given us an opportunity to speculate on relevant issues in contemporary debates about architecture and urbanism. It has provoked research into the tactics of invasion that characterise some of these

First Step: The frame
The *maquiladora*-produced metal frames are distributed at the moment of invasion. Families use them to deploy their first traces of occupation on the vacant land. The frames come equipped with prefabricated footings that can be injected into the rubber-tyre retaining walls, providing added stability.

start-up settlements, where the potential of a temporal, nomadic urbanism is supported by a very sophisticated social organisation. Hundreds of dwellers, called 'parachuters', invade, en masse, large public (sometimes private) vacant properties. As these urban guerillas parachute into the hills of Tijuana's edges, they are organised and choreographed by what are commonly called 'urban pirates'. These characters, armed with cellular phones, are the community activists who are in charge of organising the first deployment of people on the sites, as well as the community, in an effort to begin the process of requesting services from the city.

Through improvisational tactics of construction and distribution of goods and ad-hoc services, a process of assembly begins by recycling the systems and materials from San Diego's urban debris. Garage doors are used to make walls; rubber tyres are cut and dismantled into folded loops, clipped in a figure eight, and interlocked, creating a system that threads a stable retaining wall, and wooden crates make the armature for other imported surfaces, such as recycled refrigerator doors. After months of construction and community organisation, the neighbourhood begins to request services from the city. In other words, inhabitation happens first and infrastructure follows. The city sends trucks to deliver water at certain locations (one of the first infrastructural elements to be implemented is a water tank on top of some dwellings). Electricity follows as the city sends one official line, expecting the community to 'borrow' the rest via a series of illegal clippings called *diablitos* (little devils).

The sites are comprised of the stitching of these multiple situations, internal and external, simultaneously. The interiors of the dwellings become their exteriors, expressive of the history of their pragmatic evolution. As one anonymous resident put it: 'Not everything that we have is to our liking, but everything is useful.'

North to South: Disposable housing
A Tijuana speculator buys houses slated for demolition in San Diego. He puts them on wheels and brings them to the border where they will wait in line for their right to cross. Once in Tijuana they are placed on top of steel frames, leaving a space of opportunity beneath them.

It is clear that, very easily, one risks romanticising these environments and, in a sort of ethnographic gaze, patronising their fragile conditions. We cannot forget that they are the product of resistance and transgression. In a time when architecture has been so distant from the political ground and the social fabric that shapes it, the critical observation of these settlements and the assessment of possible tactics of intervention to assist their organic evolution is a risk worth taking.

In other words, the image of these informal communities' 'poverty' that planners in Tijuana and the institution of architecture want to obliterate in order to install their own project of beautification in the tabula rasa of the periphery is superseded by a sophisticated social choreography and organisation, and a temporal process of negotiating boundaries and resources. It is precisely these organisational practices and the differential systems that are invented in these environments in order to promote spatial promiscuity that can shape an alternative process of intervention in the contemporary city.

Analogous to the process of transinstitutional triangulation enacted 20 minutes away from these settlements, in San Ysidro, in order to create a microzoning strategy for Casa Familiar the Manufactured Sites project needed as a foundation a similar economic and political

Frame as Infrastructure
The frame comes with a refillable, clip-on fibre-glass water tank containing two weeks' supply.

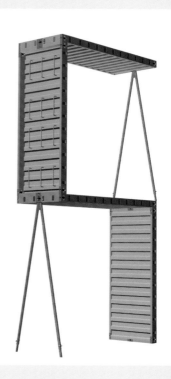

Uses of the Frame

The frame is conceived as a 'hinge' that can facilitate and strengthen the connection to the variety of recycled materials and systems. Allowing the human resourcefulness and social organisation that characterises the construction of these settlements, the frames come with a manual that can help dwellers optimise the threading of certain popular elements, such as pallet racks and recycled joists. The frame can also act as a formwork, allowing the user to experiment with different materials and finishes. And can also transform into a stair system to facilitate circulation across the difficult topography, becoming the base system for receiving some of the recycled houses from San Diego.

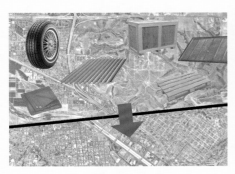

North to South: A city constructs itself from the waste of the other

Tijuana recycles a variety of materials and systems from San Diego. Discarded tyres become retaining walls. Leftover wooden pallets become dwellings. Recycled garage doors become walls and partitions. Some of these fragments are transformed into operational systems. Retaining walls made of whole tyres are further improved by the ingenuity of necessity, as people construct their own sites for inhabitation. Conventional tyres are dismantled and transformed into a system of clipped and interlocking loops to build a more solid and stable structure.

framework. In this transborder scenario, the main agencies involved are *maquiladoras* – NAFTA-supported, foreign-owned manufacturing companies, such as Sony or Samsung, operating in Tijuana to take advantage of cheap labour and low tariffs – as well as the municipality of Tijuana and an NGO, such as Casa Familiar in San Ysidro. *Maquiladora* industries have strategically positioned themselves close to informal communities of workers in Tijuana to avoid having to invest in transportation infrastructure. At this moment, there is not an official political mechanism that can monitor the transactions between *maquiladoras* and the communities they interact with to ensure some sort of social and economic equity. In other words, the CEOs of these companies are not contributing any resources to the development of minimal infrastructure needed in the informal communities that surround them.

The Manufactured Sites project proposed a collaboration between a San Diego NGO and the Municipal Planning Institute (IMPLAN) in Tijuana in order to channel funding from international foundations. Because of the formal protocol of Tijuana's

larger, interwoven and open-ended scaffolding that could help strengthen an otherwise precarious terrain, without compromising the temporal dynamics of these self-made environments. By bridging man-made and factory processes of construction the frame questions the meaning of manufacturing and of housing in the context of the community. Here, manufactured housing is not a minimalist object deployed on the ground, but an actual site, open for multiple futures.

Many lessons can still be learned from the great transnational metropolis stretching from San Diego to Tijuana, as it embraces recurring waves of a new mix of immigrants from around the world. It is out of these socio-cultural and economic tensions, and from territories of political conflict, such as this one, that critical architectural practices can emerge. These are also the transborder urban dynamics that continue to inform our work as we straddle the politics of (contaminating) zoning in San Diego, on one hand, and the tactics of invasion and the informal in

Tactics of Invasion: Start-up settlements in Tijuana
- Vacant land is 'spotted' for invasion
- 'Pirate urbaniser' organises the invasion.
- Invasion happens at dawn; invaders carry materials for start-up shelter.
- Recycled materials are incorporated.
- First consolidation takes advantage of leftover materials.
- Progressive consolidation is achieved out of social organisation.
- The local municipality begins providing services.

This 'double-sided' practice represents a pursuit for an architectural language that can be deterministic and ambiguous simultaneously, in order to frame the seemingly chaotic processes of development in many of Tijuana's nomadic settlements.

government, there is no existing model for public–private transnational collaboration to support speculative projects and help enact policy. The alliance between the municipality of Tijuana and Casa Familiar in San Ysidro has created the momentum to enact funding and policy, which would require the CEOs of the *maquiladoras* to reinvest in the communities they inhabit by sharing their own technical capabilities to facilitate minor infill infrastructure for start-up housing settlements.

In order to support this process, we are currently proposing a prefabricated *maquiladora*-produced aluminium frame that can act as a hinge mechanism to mediate the multiplicity of recycled materials and systems imported from San Diego and reassembled in Tijuana, giving primacy to the layered complexities of these sites over the singularity of the object. This frame, which can also act as formwork for a variety of positions and scenarios where a stair, pad or wall is needed, comes equipped with preassembled footings that would stitch into the existing rubber-tyre retaining walls, a bracing system that supports a plastic water pouch containing two weeks' supply, and is designed to adapt to the most popular systems that are distributed at the moment of invasion. This small piece is also the first step in the construction of a

Tijuana, on the other. This 'double-sided' practice represents a pursuit for an architectural language that can be deterministic and ambiguous simultaneously, in order to frame both the seemingly chaotic processes of development in many of Tijuana's nomadic settlements and the immigrants' tactics of encroachment into the relentless homogeneity of San Diego's picturesque order.

Can new notions of architectural form emerge out of these social formations, territorial projects whose main focus is not the object of architecture, but the subversion of the information imprinted artificially on the land, the alteration of the boundaries and limits established by the institutions of official development? A different notion of housing can emerge out of this terrain, pregnant with the promise of generating an urbanism that admits the full spectrum of social and spatial possibility. ∆

Note
1 Mike Davis, *Planet of Slums*, Verso (New York), forthcoming. Introduction published in *New Left Review*, March/April 2004. See www.newleftreview.net/NLR26001.shtml.

Housing of Contingency: Temporal urbanism

The frame's main objective is to mediate between site and house. Without compromising the improvisational energies of the communities and their temporal evolution, it adds, via a sort of urbanism of acupuncture, structural reinforcement to an otherwise precarious terrain. As the frames interconnect and are infilled by other systems, the overall system becomes a temporal scaffold that can frame the complexity of the sites. As time goes by, the frame might disappear, but only after establishing a choreography of interventions and relationships that will have given form to the new city.

HOUSE |

DWELLING IN THE NEW SOUTH AFRICA

For a country that endured decades of racial segregation, cultural freedom has a particular poignancy. Iain Low of the University of Cape Town takes his cultural barometer to the new South Africa to measure up the challenges of broadening 'the new mix' within a housing landscape that only 10 years ago was dictated by the politics of separation.

| HOME

Cohen&Judin, House Gibson, Parkview, Johannesburg, 2004
The new children's (below) and parent's (above) accommodation frames the
rear court against the original dwelling to the left.

South Africa is experiencing its 'new moment' in architecture, one
in which many cultural values are competing in the
transformation of apartheid's legacy of homogeneity and inequity.
The collapse of the artificial boundary that racially defined a
society of 'two' cultures has made space for the flowering of a
heterogeneous society. Ten years into the country's democracy,
this emerging tendency has begun to broaden the mix and extend
the range of possibilities for dwelling in the 'new' South Africa.
Not necessarily reliant upon evocative forms, this 'newness' is
predicated predominantly by the economic necessities of survival.
Architectural innovation is therefore more evident from the
production of new living arrangements that attend to the
contemporary needs of ordinary people that 'freedom' has
presented.[1]

Prior to 1994, the divisions dictated by Afrikaner Nationalist
government policy ensured a divided society characterised by
radical extremes. One of the most effective extremes arising from
such policy was that of separate development. Evident in the
spatial and formal manifestation of different architectures for the
country's black and white people, it impacted on the nature of
dwelling. Whereas the predominant aspiration of white people
was the three-bedroomed suburban house, the black equivalent
was the NE 51/9.[2] The result of research by the state's National
Building Research Institute (NBRI), the NE 51/9 was designed as an
existenzminimum for members of the black population who
qualified for residence in urban areas.

House|Home
The first decade of the post-apartheid era has been characterised
by the struggle of the African National Congress (ANC)-led
government to redress this apartheid heritage. The goal of
delivering a million houses within its first five years of
governance effected a quantitative approach to the problem of
housing. A shift in macroeconomic policy realised the
abandonment of the ANC's Reconstruction and Development
Programme (RDP)[3] in 1994 and minimalised the value of housing to
a utilitarian investment. This reductive approach has effectively
served to marginalise the production of difference that reflects
South African society.[4]

Despite the change effected by the events of 1994, the
settlement landscape of the past maintains and ensures
separation between people of ethnic difference. Evidence of
spatial dynamism is, however, an emerging phenomenon within
the confines of these historically constructed categories.
Architectural solutions consequently respond to the exigencies of
the cultural conditions that inform the lived experiences of these
(two) constituencies.

Typically, whites have located themselves in suburban
mansions or gated communities. Extending the boundary of the
private realm beyond the individual unit, these developments
reflect little desire to construct and interact with the public
realm. Social interaction and respect for commons is all but
absent. The complement to the gated community is the gated
household. Fortified architect-designed homes present
compelling edifices to a public that maintains elitist designer
lifestyles.

Notwithstanding this withdrawal to the security of privileged
environments, the responses to black communities from
government, NGOs and social-housing organisations, along with a
few private initiatives from whites, is more complex and contextual.

Row-attached units form a street edge with a generous trading sidewalk at Mansel Road.

Typical unit showing cross-sectional response with dwelling units mediated by an interior courtyard.

Typical plan configuration showing courtyards mediating the public/private spaces and the articulation of street frontage to afford formal and utilitarian resolution.

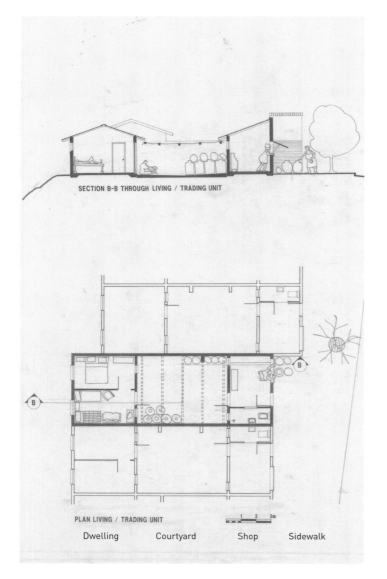

SECTION B-B THROUGH LIVING / TRADING UNIT

PLAN LIVING / TRADING UNIT

1   2   3m

Dwelling   Courtyard   Shop   Sidewalk

They present a richer set of configurations informed by two primary influences that produce their difference: economic necessity and traditional practice. These forces are interrelated, essentially expressed by accommodating the extended family through the extension of an existing dwelling, to include a rental component or a new functional space to house a small business. Consequently, such changes necessarily play themselves out in a variety of formal configurations to effect very situated architectural responses.

MANSEL ROAD, DURBAN

Architects and planners: Harber, Masson and Associates
Client: Durban City Council
Design: 1993
Implementation: 1994

Rodney Harber and his architectural practice represent a singular force in the architectural profession where there exists a consistent attempt to engage the project of transformation through all dimensions of architectural production. This endeavour has been realised through persistence and a dedication to the social dimension of architecture that appropriates the exigencies of the everyday in a productive and imaginative way. The result has been an *oeuvre* of problematic projects that are diseased with the difficulty of operating in this manner.

A response to pressure from the influx of chartered buses of rural shoppers who had begun to establish semi-permanent sidewalk homes for their weekend shopping sprees, the Mansel Road project is rich in appropriate design solutions and innovative arrangements. These are evident in the cross-programming of a public bathhouse with a commercial shop, and the shopping/dwelling units with their interior courtyard to mediate the public and private life of the family.

The project realises the opportunities inherent in urban problems, particularly in relation to empowering marginalised people and providing viable inner-city housing for poor families. By reusing wasteland, urban renewal has generated activity for both dwelling and trade. Despite its formal and design resolution, the benefits of a creative design process can be hijacked when the local authorities opt out of facilitating local/community management and delivery systems for these new structures. Though Mansel Road demonstrates the possibilities of recognising and redirecting urban conditions unique to African cities, it is evident that the process needs to be managed creatively.

Though Mansel Road demonstrates the possibilities of recognising and redirecting urban conditions unique to African cities, it is evident that the process needs to be managed creatively.

WELTEVREDE VALLEY LOW-INCOME HOUSING SCHEME, CAPE FLATS, CAPE TOWN

Architect/client: Department of Housing, Provincial
Administration of the Western Cape (PAWC)
Design: 1999
Implementation: 2000

This small greenfields insertion in Weltevrede Valley on the
Cape Flats represents a thoughtful and informed
experiment in housing design. Diverting from standard
planning regulations, it presents a dense living
environment in which vehicle usage has been marginalised,
to the benefit of its users. It relies on two complementary
strategies that contest the traditional RDP approach: a
reconfigured urban layout and multi-expandable core
dwelling units.

　　Keeping vehicles at the periphery provides for a
pedestrian-friendly interior, an environment where
children, the elderly, families and general users can find
comfort in their everyday living. The individual dwellings
are arranged in attached rows, and consist of duplex units
that have the potential to expand both vertically and
horizontally. The fixing of the interior front edge establishes
intimate streets/walkways, with kitchens fronting onto
public/play areas. The 'rear' expansion, in fact, suggests
the potential for economic units that will eventually
establish public street frontages.

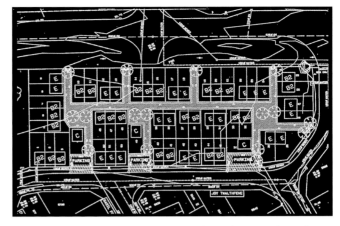

Urban neighbourhood configuration with parking at the street edge and
pedestrian/play areas at the interior.

Typical interior-street configuration
with pedestrian-scaled unit access.

Back-street elevation with first
tentative rear extensions.

This small greenfields insertion
in Weltevrede Valley on the Cape Flats
represents a thoughtful and informed
experiment in housing design. Diverting
from standard planning regulations,
it presents a dense living environment
in which vehicle usage has been
marginalised, to the benefit of its users.

Plan/section layouts
Left: Ground-floor plan with public
communal/living and service functions.
Right: Section showing mezzanine sleeping deck
and rear expansion wall.

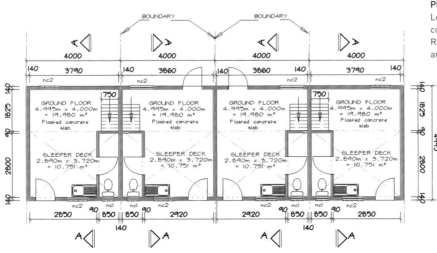

Ground-Floor plan
Scale 1:100

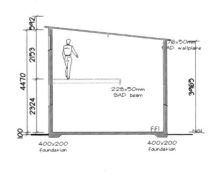

Section A-A
Scale 1:100

ELANGENI SOCIAL HOUSING, ALBERT STREET, JOHANNESBURG

Architect: Savage + Dodd Architects
Client: Johannesburg Housing Company (JHC)
Design: 1998
Implementation: 2000

Though some 1.6 million houses have been delivered in 10 years, national government housing policy has still failed to deliver both the quantity and quality of housing that meets not only the expectations of its citizens, but, more importantly, the needs of an urbanising environment. Imagination here is not a strong point. Despite ambitious policy shifts, it seems that, although there have been momentary breakthroughs, the government lacks the capacity to engage with the speculative thinking that fuels the imagination necessary to produce new living arrangements commensurate with the transformed society. The Elangeni housing project is the result of a social-housing initiative. It presents a workable example of the integration of living and working that complements the South African urban and social conditionalities. If space is to be transformed, then so, too, must be the (government) agencies that implement change. If the Afrikaner Nationalist government could establish a spatial research institute devoted to fulfilling its political vision, then a similar response is required post-apartheid.

Like the NE 51/9, Elangeni, in downtown Johannesburg, presents an alternative that is worthy of examination. It is a mixed-use, urban infill, medium-rise building that manages to achieve both diversity and densification. This in turn affords a number of real opportunities and choices that benefit occupants and the greater city alike.

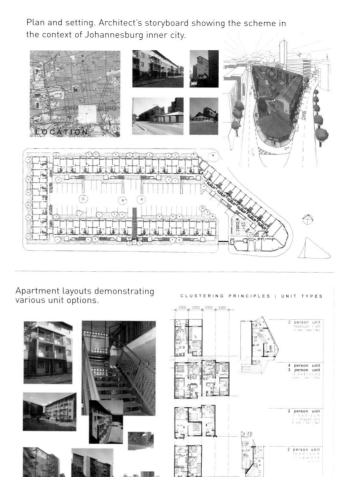

Plan and setting. Architect's storyboard showing the scheme in the context of Johannesburg inner city.

Apartment layouts demonstrating various unit options.

CLUSTERING PRINCIPLES | UNIT TYPES

Interior parking court with interactive access stairs and balconies

Live/work dwelling units at the outer edge forming an interface with the inner-city regeneration.

HOUSE GIBSON, PARKVIEW, JOHANNESBURG

Architects: Cohen&Judin
Client: Angus Gibson, Fiona Rankin-Smith
Design: 2003
Implementation: 2004

The adaptation of this suburban home in the leafy suburbs of Johannesburg contests the autonomy of the 'freestanding pavilion at the centre of the site' configuration perpetuated by suburban homes all over the world. Through a considered and careful incorporation of additional accommodation, the site has been transformed into an interactive domain, somewhat reminiscent of a traditional African kraal (village/hut). This reconfiguration has established ground for the comfortable coexistence of five competing occupants of the home: the parents, the children, the domestic worker and her family, the home/work space and guest accommodation. The outdoor space between provides the glue and mediation between what might have been conflicting arrangements on such a relatively tight site.

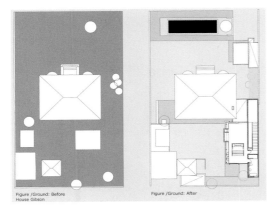

Figure /Ground: Before House Gibson

Figure /Ground: After

The reactivated site plan showing the grain of subcourtyard spaces that help to create a fieldwork of interconnection.

Original dwelling with minor amendments and a new entry, guest house and accommodation insertion to the left.

Reflective of emerging cultural practices, these few architectural expressions are not repudiations of the past, but, rather, attempts to contribute to change via careful and considered transformation of the reality that confronts South Africa. Ultimately, the task is to develop an architecture that values a located or critical heterogeneity and thereby comes to reflect the incredible diversity of the human creative.

Considering the miraculous political change for which South Africa is renowned, there is an almost universal expectation that the country should be a leader when it comes to change, especially in the field of housing. However, while it has been reasonably easy to effect change through legislation and a new constitution, the spatial legacy of apartheid presents a greater challenge. This is a condition that is further weighed down by the gravity of radical global destabilisation as well as local cultural conservatism.

The limited group of architectural practitioners contributing to the challenge of broadening the cultural landscape of housing includes fringe or counter-movements of creative individuals and collectives who are marginal to the mainstream. Pursuing strategies reliant on social thinking together with observations of cultural practice, they operate at the interstices of society. Relatively ignored by the mainstream and market, they may operate in academies, social-housing foundations or local government, as well as in private practice. Such creative thinking and making requires more support, knowledge, agility and a greater capacity to engage the contingent reality.

Reflective of emerging cultural practices, these few architectural expressions are not repudiations of the past, but, rather, attempts to contribute to change via careful and considered transformation of the reality that confronts South Africa. Ultimately, the task is to develop an architecture that values a located or critical heterogeneity and thereby comes to reflect the incredible diversity of the human creative. In attending to housing, this seems to be firmly situated in an interpretation of the home as both a social and an economic entity that supports the complex dimensions of contemporary dwelling and transcends the simplicity of a pure investment. ⌂Ɒ

Notes
1 DM Calderwood, *Native Housing in South Africa*, University of the Witwatersrand (Johannesburg), 1953.
2 I Low, 'Space and transformation/10 years – 10 buildings', *Digest of South African Architecture*, 'Space and Transformation: 10 Years of Democracy' issue, Picasso Headline (Cape Town), 2004/05.
3 African National Congress, *The Reconstruction and Development Programme: A Policy Framework*, Umanyano/ANC (Johannesburg), 1994.
4 JA Scott, *Seeing Like a State: How Certain Schemes to Improve the Human Condition Have Failed*, Yale University Press (New Haven, CT), 1998.

CENGIZ BEKTAS

AND THE COMMUNITY OF KUZGUNCUK IN ISTANBUL

The restoration of this 19th-century Ottoman house by Cengiz Bektas shows the extent of the challenge in regenerating the historic neighbourhoods of Istanbul. The house exhibits the domestic spatial order of the Istanbul house, with the major upper order on the first floor, consisting of a central stair and 'sofa' space.

Situated on the slopes of the Bosporus, Kuzguncuk is a historic suburban area of Istanbul made up of traditional Ottoman houses mixed with 20th-century apartments and terraces, though retaining the Ottoman street and block topography. Encompassing Muslim, Jewish and Christian Orthodox communities, it is a microcosm of what Istanbul has to offer. English architect **David Height**, who had the opportunity to work for Cengiz Bektas for a year in his studio in Kuzguncuk, describes Bektas's role in the regeneration of the area.

As a continuous centre of culture and society, Istanbul can claim perhaps the most concentrated, and at the same time, diverse urban history among world cities.

Despite fluctuations in fortune, a number of sieges, earthquakes and conflagrations, Istanbul has never lost its status as the crossroads of Europe and Asia, and the gateway between the Mediterranean and Black seas. A dense metropolitan population has thrived here since the city was selected as the centre of the Roman Empire in the 4th century AD, to its current incarnation, characterised by suburban agglomerations, alarming levels of pollution and an apparently haphazard approach to development.

Paradoxically, the contemporary city rarely reveals a continuity with its past. This is partly the result of the evolution of the city's metabolism over the centuries. Much of the population has shifted from historic districts along the Golden Horn or Constantinopolitan neighbourhoods, to the anonymity and modernity of the Asian centres along Bagdat Street. The business districts have migrated from the Old City, by way of the 19th-century boulevards of Beyoglu, to the dual carriageways and high-rises of Levent. Such migration has occurred over centuries, influenced by the industrialisation of the 19th and 20th centuries, the inadequacy of the ancient infrastructure to cope with modern demands and, more recently, by the migration of extraordinary numbers of the

The house in Kuzguncuk that Cengiz Bektas restored as his own home, in keeping with the neighbouring context.

Anatolian population to the city, with a virtual siege camp of squatter settlements around the edges of Istanbul.

Kuzguncuk, one of the chain of historic suburban neighbourhoods sitting on the slopes of the Bosporus, is an exception. The neighbourhood has managed to avoid both wholesale redevelopment and the stifling gentrification that increasingly devours Istanbul's remaining historic streets and timber houses. Many of these houses date from the 18th or 19th centuries. Terraces, grand city residences of the aristocracy (*konaks*) and waterfront villas (*yalis*) are unified in a spatial and urban pattern, in harmony with the family and social way of life characteristic of the Ottoman period. The grain of the neighbourhood is typical of the 18th- to 19th-century Ottoman city: steep side streets lined with bay-windowed timber houses, walled gardens, a local bathhouse, and a main tree-lined high street descending the hillside, terminating in the mesmerising flow of the Bosporus. The main street is the front door to Kuzguncuk, where bakeries, grocers, barbershops, tailors and tearooms provide for all the needs of the community. There is a palpable sense of equilibrium and longevity.

That an active mosque, synagogue and two churches (Greek and Armenian) should cohabit within Kuzguncuk's relatively small neighbourhood is easily taken for granted. The community comprises long-standing family networks, some of whom migrated from distant parts of Anatolia and others who seem to have lived in Istanbul for generations. Kuzguncuk is a microcosmic glimpse of the cosmopolitan mosaic that Istanbul is supposed to have been.

What is exceptional about Kuzguncuk is that the values of its social rootedness, its intact topography and the symbiosis between the two are recognised by many within

The open-air children's theatre at the top of Bereketli Street, on the doorstep of Gungor Dilmen, one of Turkey's leading playwrights. The street steps serve as seating.

A night-time performance of *Karagoz* (black eye) shadow puppets.

Cengiz Bektas at the centre of a neighbourhood meeting to mobilise opposition to a proposed development of the site, which is used by children as a play area.

its community. A central figure in raising this awareness and sense of civic responsibility is the architect and poet Cengiz Bektas, who has lived and worked in Kuzguncuk since the 1970s.

His practice, the Bektas Participatory Architectural Workshop, was founded on the principle of engagement with the local community to develop projects around the neighbourhood. While carrying out a substantial portfolio of works around Turkey (ultimately winning an Aga Khan Award for the Olbia University Social Centre in 2003), Bektas has devoted himself to nurturing community involvement in the regeneration of Kuzguncuk. Community participation days held over the years have led to otherwise neglected marginal spaces being landscaped or turned into artworks. Local participants are given instruction in relevant techniques (such as mural painting, or setting pebbles in cement for decorative paving), and then invited to contribute their ideas, and carry out the work. A particularly resonant intervention was the erection of an open-air stage at the top of the steps leading to the crown of Bereketli Street. Too steep for cars, the top of this street has been converted into a children's open-air theatre using the existing steps as raked seating, next to the front door of Turkey's most renowned playwright, Gungor Dilmen. Children's plays and puppet shows are held here every summer.

Bektas's mobilisation of community opinion has also resulted in a precious play area being saved from development, and a derelict building has been converted into a local library, summer school and resources centre for the community. Neighbourhood social events, which Bektas sees as vital to engendering a sense of the value of Kuzguncuk within the community, and the importance of its continued resistance to gentrification, equally play a part in the regeneration philosophy.

These projects, and the involvement of the community that has led to their realisation, are remarkable in a city where an absence of care or local engagement seems to be the rule with regard to development. Bektas lit the fuse to an otherwise dormant debate over the brutalisation of the shoreline and hillsides of the Bosporus, the automatic disregard for local communities and traditions by developers, and the general omission of landscaping or design for public amenities in Istanbul. As well as his work in Kuzguncuk, he has published numerous studies of historic towns in Anatolia, recording both the architecture of vernacular houses and the memories of local people.

His project in Kuzguncuk has attracted a community of writers, artists and academics, giving the neighbourhood a profile in many ways similar to that of the St Ives Group. All were emerging talents during the repressive years of military control in the 1970s and 1980s. Kuzguncuk has been their sanctuary. They have nurtured the next generation of Istanbul creativity. For example, Nevzat Sayin, whose practice used to occupy rooms above that of Cengiz Bektas, and Gokhan Avcioglu, both launched their careers from the Bektas workshop, and are currently leading an impressive emergence of Turkish architecture. In addition, all have, in some way, taken the question of Kuzguncuk as a starting point in their work. In the same way that the best Japanese architecture is capable of being wholly of its time, and wholly Japanese, Turkish design, they believe, should be able to fulfil its cultural potential in a similarly felicitous way.

The concept of Turkish spatial vocabulary, or a Turkish street typology, should be feasible without resort to overt historical reference. Japanese and Turkish architecture and urbanism influenced Le Corbusier and Bruno Taut, for example, and there are resonances between the way the spatial and cultural vocabulary of the Ottoman *ev* (family house – examples of which exist throughout the Balkans and Anatolia) could speak to architecture today in the same way that the *sukiya*, or teahouses, of Kyoto continue to inform the architecture of Japan. The private rooms in an Ottoman family house, flanked by an entire wall of storage space, were used for dining, sleeping or working. The floor, its covering and the divans or niches surrounding it were particularly significant as the place for sitting, sleeping and reclining. The social and family order was matched by the spatial order of the upper residential levels of the house, where rectilinearity was achieved via intricate corbelling-out from the irregular ground-level footprint, and the most private cellular rooms opened onto the open and communal 'sofa' space. In the works of Bektas and Sayin,

A ballet performance in the community learning centre Cengiz Bektas converted from a derelict building.

for example, the spatial anatomy of many of their residential projects centres on open communal volumes, off which more private secluded rooms open. The clear assembly of room volumes in their work, and their expression through the envelope of the building, resonates with the articulation of the vernacular and state architecture of the Ottomans.

Yet the majority of postwar development has simply ignored the cultural dimension of this architecture, or latched onto motifs and forms without interpreting the much deeper context. The Kuzguncuk regeneration offers an approach from the contextual rather than the formal starting point. Albeit incremental, modest and almost nonarchitectural, the reconnection of community, space and design has led to an example of culturally rooted and socially inclusive regeneration, of which many cities would be envious, and of which Istanbul should take note. ∆

As an example of contemporary architecture working with the spatial traditions of the Ottoman house, Nevzat Sayin's Emre Sanan House in Dikili shows the arrangment of rooms opening to, and oriented around, the central semipublic 'sofa'.

The subject of this article was inspired by a lecture given by Cengiz Bektas on 'Uniting the Traditional and the Contemporary', at the Royal Academy of Arts in London in February 2005, as part of the academy's architecture programme.

BUILDING TRADITIONS

THE BENNY W REICH CULTURAL CENTER FOR THE ETHIOPIAN COMMUNITY, YAVNEH, ISRAEL

Ruth Palmon describes how a hybrid high-tech mud structure in Yavneh, Israel, designed by Israeli architect Ilan Pivko, creates a lively cultural centre and synagogue for a Jewish Ethiopian community.

Front view of the cultural centre. On the ground floor, a community room opens to the plaza, and on the first floor is an introverted round synagogue reminiscent of traditional Ethiopian synagogues.

Like a design oasis, the Benny W Reich Cultural Center emerges in between the mundane housing projects of Yavneh, a small town 25 kilometres south of Tel Aviv. Yavneh is a fast-growing, dynamic and extremely diverse town, but its old shabby core stands as a reminder of the town's less fortunate past. Less than 30 years ago, a local grass-roots activist Meir Shitrit (currently serving as minister of transportation) was elected mayor at the age of 24, and instigated a miraculous process of urban and economic renewal. Today, after most of its original residents have moved to better and newer neighbourhoods, the town's core is populated mostly by Ethiopian and Russian immigrants, and the town of Yavneh is again faced with the challenges of immigration absorption and social gaps. The cultural centre, funded by the Jewish Agency for Israel, serves as a synagogue for the insular Ethiopian community who live in its immediate vicinity, but also provides after-school activities that are open to all.

To say that the centre sticks out in downtown Yavneh would be a gross understatement. Formally, it is simply striking: four mud-like parallel walls, lined with concrete benches, are placed in front of the building. Thin round timber spans between the walls, creating stripes of shade that dance on the rich texture of the mud walls. Curved overlapping walls, with the same muddy rich texture, emerge on the first floor. This ensemble of mud and sticks is held together by a pristine grey box, shaped by refined concrete formwork. The formwork leaves a trace on the centre's walls – an abstract grid of 2 x 2 metres. In contrast, the mud walls have a deep sensual texture unmistakably created by hand – an endless field of merging handprints. Thus, the small building presents a dichotomy of architectural form: abstract-technological-modern-concrete against anthropomorphic-handmade-primitive-mud.

The centre's plan is simply organised: activity rooms are located on the ground floor – a large multipurpose dividable space and two classrooms – and on the first floor is a synagogue. The synagogue and activity rooms are contained in a large, grey concrete box. The entrance to the centre is placed on the side of this box, enclosed by a clear glass curtain-wall. On the other side of the glass entrance,

a smaller concrete box holds various service spaces, such as bathrooms, offices and lifts. Thus a programmatic rhythm is created: 'main concrete box, glass entrance, service concrete box'. The mud-like elements, confined to the main box, help to establish the centre's relationship with the plaza in front of it. On the ground level, parallel mud walls extend from its main space, enclosing three sets of sliding doors. When the doors are open, the large activity room flows out to the plaza through intermediate shed-like spaces, lined with benches and covered with wood twigs. The curved mud walls of the first-floor synagogue are also lined with built benches, but since the walls overlap each other, one is prevented from directly looking outside. Light slithers through slot windows in between the walls, accentuating their deep texture and creating a comforting, warm, introverted space.

The soft interior of the synagogue attempts to invoke the round interiors of traditional Ethiopian synagogues. The mud-like walls stand for a tradition that is kept mostly by the community's elders. Every weekend and holiday, this small synagogue is packed with worshippers from the local Ethiopian community. Prayers in two shifts are common, due to lack of space, but also because the younger generation prays in Hebrew, whereas the elders pray in Amharic. On weekdays, the centre is taken over by neighbourhood teenagers and children who participate in a variety of after-school activities. 'The gap between the two cultures is tremendous,' says Gidon, age 34, a youth instructor and the director of the centre, while we tour the building together on a weekday afternoon. Back in Ethiopia, Gidon explains, life might have been modest, maybe even primitive, but everyone was in complete charge of his life, his land, his family. In Israel things are very different; mortgages, bureaucracy, no future without proper education – life is a lot more complicated.

Of all the immigrant groups Israel has absorbed over the last hundred years, the Ethiopian community's experience was perhaps the most difficult. In 2004, 20 years after the first wave of Ethiopian Jews was brought secretly to Israel in an operation named 'Moses', drug abuse, vandalism, crime rate and school-dropout statistics in the community are alarming. Aside from an actual culture shock, the Ethiopian community was faced with prejudice and distrust by governmental institutions, as well as by their average Israeli neighbour. In fact, most Ethiopians still live in segregated neighbourhoods in small peripheral towns and do not

The centre was built for the Ethiopian community as part of an effort to mitigate their absorption hardships. Yavneh is continuously and actively dealing with such absorption; it has absorbed several waves of immigration over the last 50 years.

The walls in front of the centre are an element that recalls Ethiopian traditional building methods. They create semishaded spaces covered with wood twigs that mediate the ground-floor community room and the large plaza in front of it.

A man prays facing Jerusalem, on the synagogue's fire exit. Ethiopian building traditions, represented by elements such as mud-like walls and wood twigs, are set against contemporary concrete construction. This construction culture-clash can be analogous to the Ethiopian community position in Israeli society. However, the centre doesn't merely represent Ethiopian culture, it enables its continuation in modern Israel.

Experiments in building actual mud walls were made by the architect, but weather conditions in Israel did not permit such construction. The rich texture of the mud-like wall was achieved by hand-treating a thick layer of plaster laid over concrete masonry units.

The centre was warmly embraced by Ethiopian youths in Yavneh. Although ostensibly indifferent to traditional Ethiopian elements, they recognise its unique architectural shape and take pride in it.

Inside, the centre functions like any other cultural centre. The ground-floor spaces are used for informal gatherings, after-school activities, are rented out for private parties, and also function on weekends and holidays as overflow spaces for the synagogue.

mix with other communities. Inside this small and tight community, a multitude of identities were formed. The elders in general stick to the traditional tribal culture brought from Ethiopia. They pray and speak in Amharic, and follow their spiritual leaders, the Kesim. The mid-generation, who immigrated at a young age and many of whom were brought up in boarding schools, pray in Hebrew according to Israeli traditions, and mix with those outside the community more easily. The Ethiopian youth, born and raised in secular modern Israel, have rejected, in many cases, their parents' traditional ways. Yet young Ethiopians are not always embraced by Israelis, and many of them have found an alternative identity through black music, thus creating an Afro-Israeli subculture, complete with its own rap groups, black-music clubs and a culture of protest. Gidon, being a member of the mid-generation, is not enthusiastic about Israeli-Ethiopian-black culture. In his opinion, identifying with Afro-Americans is simply a way for young people to channel frustration and anger.

When I ask Gidon how young people feel about the mud walls, he maintains that it is important to preserve and respect the old tradition. Later in the afternoon, three

The synagogue is used solely by Ethiopians on weekends and holidays. Prayers are held in Amharic as well as in Hebrew. The round, soft introverted interior is reminiscent of traditional Ethiopian synagogues.

teenage girls dressed in pink, baby blue and bright red, with back packs and in an elevated mood, storm into the centre and camp out in Gidon's office. Teasing and joking like teenage girls do in the presence of their older youth guide, they argue and brag about who is living in the worst neighbourhood, and complain about the fact that their high-school library construction was stopped due to financial problems. Then they express their unmediated opinions about the centre: 'Smashing! The best building in the whole town – this is practically our second house,' they exclaim. The conversation is interrupted when a Russian couple enters the centre enquiring about the possibility of renting the space for a party.

While seemingly indifferent to the symbolic architectural gesture of a fragile tradition contained in a Modernist frame, the girls are obviously aware, and proud of the fact, that this is a good building. Gidon thinks that a good building is good for the community; it gives them a sense of importance and something to be proud of. His eyes lit up when he recited the words of the architect, Ilan Pivko, that the mud walls, the Ethiopian tradition, are like a jewel in a concrete jewel box.

Pivko is mostly known in Israel for his high-end residential work and fashionable club designs. Growing up in a state of culture clash himself, between a European immigrants' house and the Israeli melting pot, he is intrigued by oppositions in general, and preoccupied with cultural oppositions in particular. Sitting in his

A good building is good for the community; it gives them a sense of importance and something to be proud of. The mud walls, the Ethiopian tradition, are like a jewel in a concrete jewel box.

The synagogue is a protected enclave of Ethiopian culture. Its curved mud-like walls slightly overlap, preventing a direct view of the outside, yet allowing soft light to slither along them, accentuating their texture.

posh office in the gentrified part of old Jaffa, he explains how he wanted the Ethiopian cultural centre architecture to harmoniously unite the Ethiopian and Israeli cultures. The Israeli so-called 'melting pot' – an attitude that emerged in the 1950s and aspired to create a new Israeli identity devoid of any traces of diaspora culture, also became the local ideological drive behind the International Style in Israeli architecture. While many deserving buildings were built in Israel under Modernism, it also reinforced a certain European cultural hegemony. Pivko represents a different generation, with a more diverse and sensitive cultural attitude, and possibly marks an important direction in Israeli architecture.

When faced with the challenge of designing for the Ethiopian community in Israel, Pivko decided to bring together two building traditions – traditional Ethiopian straw-and-mud construction and contemporary Israeli cast-concrete construction. In search of an authentic Ethiopian construction tradition, he conducted mud-construction experiments with Ethiopians who brought the knowledge from their motherland. Unfortunately, technical difficulties were not overcome, and as mud seemed to be melting

in the Mediterranean rain, mud walls were represented by concrete masonry unit (CMU) walls covered with hand-treated plaster. This fragile representation of African vernacular architecture is carefully contained in an architectural representation of contemporary Israel – technological, rational, clean, colourless.

At first sight, these two architectural forms seem so remote from one another, alien, artificially glued together, that one cannot avoid thinking of this building as a grim metaphor for an irreconcilable culture clash. On closer inspection, it becomes apparent that for the community that uses the building, while experiencing an everyday complex cultural reality, simplified metaphors become invisible. For them, the Benny W Reich Cultural Center is a harmonious, well put together, 'smashing' building. ⚙

The photography for this article was specially shot for this issue of ᴆ by Jerusalem-based photo-journalist Ahikam Seri, whose work displays a particular preoccupation with the social and cultural. www.ahikamseri.com

MAKING PLACE IN
BANGALORE

In the city of Bangalore in southern India, the predominant architectural language is that of conventional global commerce. 'Bland high-rise developments' jostle with shanties and urban sprawl. Anooradha Iyer Siddiqi, AIA, explores an alternative way, by Shilpa Sindoor Architects and Planners. The practice invests in a sense of place, but also uses a knowledge of the local construction market and materials to its economic advantage.

According to a UN report released in 2004,[1] by 2007, for the first time in history, more than half the world's population will live in urban areas. The most radical growth will occur in developing countries, where two-fifths of the urban population will live in slums, significantly challenging already overburdened infrastructure and scarce resources.

The new culture in the megacities of South Asia combines both the latest iteration of Asia's relationship to the Occident and the self-assurance of imminent superpower status. As edges of the cultural mosaic blur into a commercial melting pot, wayward architectural descendants of the International Style proliferate across the cityscape. While architecture in the language of Chandigarh or Dhaka heralded a proud, modern, discrete yet egalitarian culture, today's social blend is signified by sprawling amorphous urban form in cities undifferentiated within themselves and indistinct from each other.

Bangalore, the South Indian city frontlining the cybertechnology boom, illustrates the physical and cultural conditions of the new South Asian city. Since India liberalised its markets in the early 1990s and began to encourage trade and foreign investment, this Silicon Valley competitor has weathered a property boom and increased in population by almost 2 million. The city is negotiating one of the conundrums of unprecedented urban growth in the developing world – adjacent conditions of extreme poverty, extreme wealth and a booming middle-class, with the attendant architectural expressions of each. The mild climate and picturesque image of the low-rise garden city (once lush with old-growth trees and peppered with clay-tiled colonial bungalows) is now threatened by air pollution, sprawl, bland high-rise development and dense interstitial occupancies (namely sidewalk small-businesses and slum shanties). Roads, public transport and urban infrastructure never grew to meet the expansion of the last decade.

During the early 1990s, new construction ringed the city's dense core, only for empty building shells to dominate the landscape during the economic downturn at the end of the decade, surrounded by the 'soft' architecture of squatter camps morphing at their bases. The monumental concepts of Chandigarh and centralised planning of medieval temple cities like Madurai have no civic relevance in this situation. Bangalore's predominant architecture is not invested in place – because it is temporary, out of scale, out of character or simply parasitic in nature, existing as an artefact of speculative development.

In response to these conditions, or perhaps despite them, architects are rooting local architecture, even temporary construction, in place. Bangalore practice Shilpa Sindoor reinterprets local traditional construction methods and building types. It relies on resources available specifically in this region, tying its projects to the land by default. By experimentally manipulating materials outside the common usage, the firm questions normative structural design and tests alternative construction methods within a familiar frame of reference. This recasting of building traditions and techniques has the potential to evoke the quality of a region without being beholden to a unique site or historical context. Within the event of rapid 'place-making' (as architects are increasingly being approached to design entire towns), a compelling alchemy of Modernism and traditional vernacular construction emerges that suggests new definitions of regionalism in architecture.

Shilpa Sindoor architects Shankar and Navnath Kanade trace the next step in the subcontinent's Modernist path, branching uniquely from the family tree of Le Corbusier, Louis Kahn and Balkrishna Doshi (a founder of modern South Asian architectural practice and education). They propose a new blend of regional vernacular grammar with a modern spatial vocabulary. Within the structure of the *plan libre*, they have designed an inexpensive, low-tech system of sustainable building that yields a sectional variety, provides harmony with nature, encourages an active urban life and responds to historical context. The innovative technology realises both a traditional reliance on locally available materials and an ideal modern aesthetic.

Shilpa Sindoor's pioneering construction hinges on a reduction in high-cost materials and a reliance on low-cost labour. The standard building technology in most of South Asia is a concrete slab and column frame, concrete footings and foundations, flat slab roofs, and walls of brick infill and plaster cover. Production of cement for use in slabs, columns and plaster is costly, energy-intensive and polluting. In the region of Bangalore, lime (a locally extracted organic resource) is a less expensive alternative to cement, but suffers from a significantly slower curing rate that does not meet the demands of fast-tracked construction projects. Masonry, specifically rough-cut granite quarried locally, provides an economical alternative to concrete frame and plastered-brick infill walls, since production of kiln-fired brick strains the same energy resources as cement and the quality of sun-dried brick is not easily controlled or standardised. Stone, unlike brick, does not require a two- to three-coat plaster cover to prevent weathering and hold paint finish. By leveraging an increased percentage of project cost into labour rather than materials, the architects have driven down prices by up to a

Shilpa Sindoor, Keremani Apartments, Bangalore, 1999
The apartment block under construction. The vertical slab construction presents an alternative to the structural principle of stacking.

third of the cost of similar-sized projects dependent upon standard construction, without depending on a skilled work force or complex custom building systems. All the technology is based on simple building practices that any mason knows, and the system is gentle on the natural environment.

The hybrid masonry system begins with a four-leaf-clover-shaped block with a hole in the centre, cured from a lime and cement compound. (Lime is mixed with a limited quantity of cement and aggregate to reduce construction time and project cost.) These blocks are stacked vertically in increments of 3 feet, laid with mortar, and trued via the centre hole with reused steel from the site (for example, remnants of the reinforcing bar from

Shilpa Sindoor, Lohitaswa Family House, Bangalore, 1992
View from a high bedroom opening overlooking an interior court through the full depth of the zoned site. Spatial continuity and the view expand the horizon of a tight space. Figured rough-cut granite is one of the cheapest building materials in the region, and stone quality consistently precludes the need for custom selection.

Shilpa Sindoor building site. Coordination of curing times and phased building with alternating masonry and concrete systems creates complex project management conditions, overcome by the abundance of migrant labour. Workers are often employed as entire families, with women (at lower pay rates) constituting the bulk of the work force. Construction sites are often playgrounds for labourers' children, places where their parents forge an ironically domestic realm.

Shilpa Sindoor, Lohitaswa House, Bangalore, 1992
The open courts of this family house move light and air through the building. The environmental controls depend solely on 'passive' means: materials that are slow to gain heat, ventilation via an interlocking system of open-air volumes, with sunlight penetrating the depth of the space.

slab pours) and a consistent grout pour. The scrap steel provides a dowel connection for the next 3-foot increment of column, and the channels formed on four sides of the stacked clover brick grip vertically laid granite slabs, also jointed with mortar. Such slabs are typically pre-cut en masse for sidewalk cover of water and waste lines to a size that two labourers can carry. The phased interlocking system of columns and granite panels provides stabilisation in the vertical direction, and a design of multiple split levels within the buildings allows the slab frequent horizontal tie-ins with the masonry system. The principle of dramatically varying the section also provides spatial variety and allows free movement of light and air through the space. All the materials are natural and durable, and locally available, which alleviates cost and fuel burdens on shipping.

In the Keremani apartment housing and Lohitaswa single-family residence projects, the open plan is organised around a series of courts that expand the interior vista, revealing the full depth of a built plot. The progression up through the building is via floor levels that engage the voids of these courts at each half-storey. Walls are minimised, and privacy is achieved through sectional differentiation. The three-dimensional compositions balance exaggerated lines of struck mortar joints, the Brutalist topography of

Moonlight in the Lohitaswa House.

Shilpa Sindoor building block – the seed.

Shilpa Sindoor, Lohitaswa House, Bangalore, 1992
Left: Light and shadows are framed in a small granite slab-walled court.
Right: An open-air granite court houses a garden.

rough-cut figured grey granite and finished black slate, and planes of red colour (sealed wire-cut brick and iron-oxide flooring, a low-cost concrete sealant applied in a labour-intensive manual process).

In the hot months, room temperatures dip almost 20°F due to the stone and concrete material of the walls and floors. The often open-air mosquito-netted courts passively ventilate the interior by drawing hot air up and out of the buildings, and serve as light wells for the adjacent spaces. These spaces often open directly onto the courts, with no weather-sealing. The architects stand philosophically on the side of living directly within the local ecosystem, experiencing weather, fauna, and the movement of the sun and moon within the walls of home.

The relationship between hard architecture and vegetation in the interior courts of these projects finds a larger expression in the urban landscape of the Jal Vayu Vihar town plan outside the city centre. The primary construction material for this entire complex is a rough-cut granite rubble, stacked in courses using a traditional masonry construction method. The stone acts as a static backdrop for flowers, vines and potted plants that cover the landscape. Tree-lined avenues, large public spaces, and small intimate outdoor rooms and gardens vary the quality of the urban environment.

Locally quarried granite slabs span ditches dug for water and waste lines. Like ice in the tundra and sand in the desert, the abundance of stone in this region inspires structural experimentation, in this case setting a building material in tension that is typically used in compression.

Making place presents the challenge of addressing scale. Spatial variety in the streets and roofscape result from a design in which every apartment is laid out uniquely in plan and section. Both indoor and outdoor spaces carve away at the granite blocks, recalling both functional aspects of village vernacular architecture in South India and the modern spatial sensibilities of Loos. The ancient Indian town-planning principle of a landmark square is reborn here in a sculptural centralised water tank that

Shilpa Sindoor, Jal Vayu Vihar, Bangalore, 1991
The landscape of roofs at Jal Vayu Vihar, a planned town on the periphery of Bangalore. Service ladders shelter water and waste pipes. (The photo predates the growth of flowering vines on the stone.)

All the materials are natural and durable, and locally available, which alleviates cost and fuel burdens on shipping.

The habitable roofscape of Karnataka village, near Bangalore. Life takes place on roofs as much as in the street. People wash clothes, dry food and sleep at night on the tops of their homes.

Cantilevering stone treads trace a path to the roof in Karnataka village, near Bangalore.

echoes the elemental forms and voids of Kahn's work on the subcontinent. Sculpted forms are mirrored by sculpted light that shapes much of the experience of passage through the streets and alleys of the project.

The essays in construction, town planning, sustainability, urban form, space and light are met by a foray into the almost mystical realm of making community. The designers had to meet the social and architectural concerns of a diverse populace. Jal Vayu Vihar encourages a vibrant urban life, with interconnecting spaces at street level, on stairs to the roofs, and in connections between roofs of various buildings that are independent from the street. The layout encourages independent (often gender-based) communities to develop on the street level and at the roof level, and a security policy of 'eyes on the street', much as Jane Jacobs described.[2] Its design also considered housing for migrant worker communities as part of town-planning phasing and general construction staging, with diverse nodes and centres allowing for the possibility of both speculative and temporary development, making a place for both the 'hard' architecture of buildings and the 'soft' architecture of platforms, tents and shanties.

The charge of architects in South Asia and other rapidly developing urban areas is complex. As is the case anywhere, in the rush to get something built it is almost inconceivable to actually attempt a meaningful architecture. The pace at which cities grow does not devalue institutional and personal connection to the built environment, but dictates new means of exercising that connection. Survival in the global village and the ballooning city has demanded that the new citizens evolve beyond, or deny, language, caste, religion, ethnicity, gender, economic class, custom and habit. In a land where regional traditions are thousands of years strong, these conditions jeopardise the meaning of 'place' and render acts of territorialisation bereft of any significance other than political. This phenomenon is exaggerated by information technology's triumph of meaningful virtual place over physical place.

Mix in the urban environment was always symptomatic of a guerilla movement that surreptitiously and unpredictably thwarted the surveillance nature of the master plan, as in the production of the 'illegal' slums, and the continuous bending of urban rules and regulations that made up the master plan. Without the disciplinary deployment of the master plan, and even within it, a city will always rearrange itself to ever new arcs of desire, to new tribal, economic and cultural orientations. Lutyens' New Delhi, and Le Corbusier's Chandigarh, share a common criticism that they disavow the inherent mix of Indian cities and curtail any impromptu, hybridising intervention (although the architecture of both is better understood as a work of cultural syncretism).

Every epoch brings its own poetry of mix, and every hybridity is distinctive. A new mix is certainly redefining the contemporary urban landscape in South Asia in ways that are unprecedented and not fully predicated on home-spun norms. If an earlier mix was of the Hobson-Jobson variety, triggered either by colonial infraction or metropolitan-rural polarity, the new mix is engineered by a triad of forces – transnational culture, new media and intoxicating consumerism. There is as yet no Shanghai syndrome in Indian/South Asian cities, a mad rush to build from the triadic forces, but nevertheless all cities are undergoing paroxysmal changes. It is far from clear whether the new landscape, with new works of architecture, is a culturally liberating mode or a surreptitious profit-driven product. Is the mix only spectacular, or does it promise social justice? Is it truly a mix, or a juxtaposition of attitudes and desires that are tangential to each other, in reality maintaining a wedge between the various constituencies? Will the new triad transcend the deep cut of the religious divide, and offer a new urban promise for Amar, Akbar and Anthony: the metrosexual metropolis?[2]

Mixed Blessing

Masala, originally a culinary term for stewing spices, has now entered the Anglo-Indian vocabulary as an ideogram of amalgamation. What the 'melting pot' is to the American sensibility, masala is to the South Asian imaginary, alluding both to a mix and a potent, spicy content. This culinary sensibility has now travelled to a wider body of work. The film industry in Mumbai – Bollywood, which perhaps should now be called Mollywood in accordance with the city's name change – employs the term as a tool for concoction and exaggeration. In *Mississippi Masala*, the film-maker Mira Nair alludes to the new racial and cultural coagulation on the banks of the Mississippi. Canadian film *Masala* follows the displaced god Krishna from the bowery of Vrindaban to a video shrine amidst the discordant coordinates of diasporic Indians in Toronto. And Salman Rushdie, in his various novels, employs the masala mode in his characterisations and imageries, and especially in the spoken language, as a

Uttam Kumar Saha, Reza House, Dhaka, 2000–02
A tropical bricolage.

Rajeev Kathpalia, Vastu Shilpa Consultants, Arjun Farmhouse, Ahmedabad, 2004
The 'farmhouse' is the site of a new architectural exuberance.

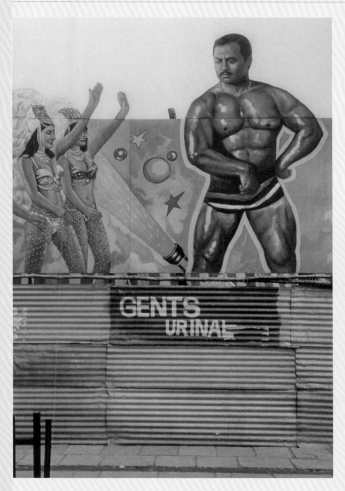
Urban montage: street scene, Delhi.

Urbana Architects, Lalmatia Apartments, Dhaka, 2004
The interior is an assemblage of the machine-made, handcrafted and resurrected.

Life in Sundarnagar, the make-believe Indian town in the film *Mein Prem Ki Diwani Hoon*, which was actually shot in New Zealand.

If mix and hybridity are the new mantras that will dislodge the power of the pure and unitary, we are not yet sure whether it is eventually going to be redemptive or disruptive.

Hafeez Contractor, DLT-DT3 City Center, Gurgaon, 2002
The embodiment of elsewhere: the mall as an exotic destination.

Postmodern vitality. It is this vitality and hybridity that threaten the grip of the Classical and the thoroughbred traditional, as well as the squeaky-clean modern.

Fusion and remix are now the cultural engines from Mumbai to Macao, especially as they are spewed out non-stop through ubiquitous TV channels. In music, new genres are being configured by an invigorating and sometimes unabashed miscegenation that preys on the techniques of 'remix'. The infinite mixing capability of the camera and digital media – like the fast output of a TV commercial that in three seconds will flicker 30 images of diverse provenance – has taken collage or montage to a new height. The phenomenon is quite widespread: for example, A Samia Farah, a Tunisian singer who sings in French employing jazz, reggae and hip hop. Musical remix may be a metaphor for a larger reality where life or culture is no longer whole. It is composed of the simultaneous existence of multiple realities, of bits and pieces of both the familiar and the strange, and it does not matter whether they add up to a whole, or whether the bits and pieces are themselves constantly in flux.

If mix and hybridity are the new mantras that will dislodge the power of the pure and unitary, we are not yet sure whether it is eventually going to be redemptive or disruptive. Where the new mix differs from Bhabha's idea of hybridity is that it is not necessarily situated in 'in between' spaces (that is, the cracks and fissures of official spaces), but constitutes its own spatial matrix in the urban landscape. The term hybrid still refers to some kind of originary pureness, and suggests an eventual upturning,

Hafeez Contractor, Dheeraj Dreams development, Bhandup, ongoing
Developing a dream topography.

and therein lies its valorised status. The new mix announces a posthybrid moment whence the binary of hybridity/purity and abnormality/normativity does not have to be resorted to. The new mix constitutes its own terms of reference.

A Place Called Elsewhere

In the 2003 film *Mein Prem Ki Diwani Hoon*, the setting is a fictional town eponymously called Sundarnagar, or 'the city beautiful'. It is a town of idealised dreams and bourgeois opulence, of houses belonging to the purveyors of traditions, with living rooms the size of convention halls, populated by pampered patriarchs, gullible grandmothers and servile servants, all in their proper places. The lawns to the houses are wide, and the driveways regal, while the mellifluous town harbours manicured parks, quaint telephone booths, gardens, and outdoor spaces to run away to that include quite inexplicably snow-clad mountains, lush streams and sandy beaches, all in one go. In the film, Sundarnagar is depicted as a town in India, yet the entire film was shot in New Zealand. The Indian city of Sundarnagar may be fictive, but it is depicted in a real place. That place is elsewhere, and this is the ubiquitous trope in Hindi-Bollywood films: the relentless flight towards elsewhere.

This flight to elsewhere is structurally embedded in the song-dance numbers – the '*chansons d'amour*' – that are the *raisons d'être* of Hindi-Bollywood films. I call the location of these *chansons d'amour* song-sites. The song-site in the Hindi-Bollywood filmic imagination weaves music, dance, couture, urban and landscape imagery into a phantasmagoria of dreams and desires. The literal space of such song-sites has always been an exotic, faraway place, somewhere the inevitable amorous couple could instantly be transported to without

Hafeez Contractor, Apartment Towers for Mumbai, 2000
Urban towers: an ensemble of styles, genres and desires.

Hafeez Contractor,Lake Castle development, Powai, Mumbai, 1989
Signatures of a new living: mixed metaphors and stratospheric locations.

a cue. The lush valley of Kashmir was a ubiquitous site of that dream topography, as also are places like Manali, Kanyamumari, Goa and Simla. But now, more and more, since Kashmir has devolved into a political chaos or the transnational siren has finally arrived, the song-sites exist subliminally in imported places, in Switzerland, Germany, even New Zealand. As in a veritable catalogue of the *National Geographic* exotica, charming, picturesque, urbane or just generally well-formed places are grafted onto the body of an extremely predictable, rebarbative and supertheatrical narrative that may have a generic setting in some *gaon* in Punjab, or a *chawl* in Mumbai. What makes *Mein Prem* striking is that it is in its entirety a song-site; it takes the elsewhere of the song-site to the entire film.

What to make of the manufacture of this cinematic urban imagery without being facetious? Can one make an Italo Calvino-like catalogue of these grafted places, as a kind of modern fable of urban imagination? Or, can they be treated as a cryptic enumeration of the collective fetish of the Indian urban middle-class as it encounters, experiences and succumbs to (new) global coordinates? Or, are these sites a symptom of a Postmodern hybridity (a new mix) manufactured, distributed and consumed filmically? Or, is Bollywood, surreptitiously, unwittingly or unselfconsciously, writing alternative visions for urban India? Or, is cinematic Sundarnagar, as Thomas Pynchon did with the medium of TV in his fictional work *Vineland*, a 'quixotic cognitive enterprise' that converts a Postmodernist space into a tool for thinking about an otherwise elusive and unrepresentable system?[3]

With quixotic Sundarnagar we are in the realm of urban images and imageries, no matter whether they are from a non-reflexive cultural production, and no matter whether they are props in a substance-denuded performance. A new expressive congruence is formed nonetheless by cinema, architecture and spatial utopia which now enter the realm of imagining the city. These places from elsewhere, real and actual, become fictive in the Hindi film narrative because the places are not named, and they are not located with any amount of precision; they are literally framed to be 'foreign', to be elsewhere. It is this admixture of actuality and alienness that makes these sites hyper-real places. In generic Hindi films, the sites of the songs are hyper-real because they are seemingly real. The sites are not unreal by themselves. A city like that exists somewhere in Germany. A landscape like that exists in Switzerland. And yet they become profoundly unreal or, if you prefer, seemingly real, and hence hyper-real, by the nature of being grafted on the cinematic body, when they are collaged, montaged, cut-and-pasted alongside a normative and urbanistically messy landscape – a real city in India. The significance is in the juxtaposition, in the being side by side.

What is being side by side? The normative and the superlative, the usual and the ideal, the place here and now, and a place elsewhere. It is technically a juxtaposition of the messy landscape and dream topography. The former is of a native and the latter of a transnational provenance. It is also in this sense that spaces of Hindi film represent a 'mix'. And despite what is perhaps conceptually a jarring hybridity, the satisfied audience takes it as a 'flow', a flow through diverse, unrelated, discontinuous spaces. Sundarnagar is not an isolated cinematic place, and yet Sundarnagar is not an Indian town that could be located with precision for it is part of the longing of the urban upper-/middle-class to approximate an 'elsewhere'. And yet we do not know whether that longing is therapeutic or psychotic.

What distinguishes Sundarnagar from another well-known fictional town – RK Narayan's Malgudi – is the transnational divide, the trope of consumptive desire embedded scene-by-scene in the former, in the frame-by-frame embodiment of transnational utopias on the native set of reference, of the presence of the idea of a globally charged place that replaces (or at least contests) the last vestiges of the empirical here. Is Sundarnagar, then, a premonition of Indian cities – part of a narrative on urban imagination in India – happening in the simultaneous collapse of either Nehruvian or Gandhian ideology, and the proliferation of a global, transnational indulgence?

The Metrosexual Mantra

The longing for 'elsewhere' is now embodied in new building configurations that are radically altering the urban landscape: malls and shopping centres, cineplexes and flyovers, and exclusive apartment or residential complexes. The shoppers and strollers at Connaught Place in New Delhi have literally gone elsewhere, abandoning the old commercial centre for more exclusive, air-conditioned enclaves that are spread out as a matrix of hyperspace in the familiar landscape. Billboards of upcoming shopping centres in and around Calcutta rise from the ashen and smoky landscape of the city like some divine promise. The gigantic Basundhara City, which is not a city but touted as Asia's largest mall, has replaced the

> The longing for 'elsewhere' is now embodied in new building configurations that are radically altering the urban landscape: malls and shopping centres, cineplexes and flyovers, and exclusive apartment or residential complexes.

traditional site of promenade and vicarious assembly for the people of Dhaka. At Nagpur Airport, I discovered the model and rendered drawing of an apartment complex as not so much the bourgeois dream house as we know it, but of an enigmatic collective future. Frederic Jameson's rumination on the hyperspatial quality of certain Postmodern spaces, such as the atrium of the Bonaventure Hotel in Los Angeles, comes to mind. While these spaces are here upon us, for us to travel to and enter, we do not possess, as Jameson warns, 'the perceptual equipment to match this new hyperspace'.[4]

In this new, urban admixture, an architect like

Balkrishna Doshi is already exiled in Malgudi, in a pre-consumerist and anti-transnational ethos, while someone like Hafeez Contractor has taken on the mantle of translating the dream of elsewhere in many projects and images that could be strung together as a veritable chutney of architectural history. Doshi's vision for New Jaipur, a city premised on the historic nature of urban amalgamation, seems already dated, and overly 'real'. Hafeez Contractor is now the 'world famous' architect from India, getting coverage in a whole issue of the Indian magazine *Architecture+Design* (Jan/Feb 2003). He has replaced the self-reflexive practice to become the architectural doyen of the euphoric and uncertain present.

It would not be an exaggeration to describe the mall as the urban space *par excellence*, born out of a transnational breeding that, on the one hand, represents the shopping experience of America and, on the other, embodies the surreal city of Sundarnagar. While the South Asian malls are typologically derivative of those in the US, the internal coding of the latter are reworked in the South Asian context. While US malls are populist destinations, the mall in India/South Asia has taken on a unique upscale and exclusive aura that is codified by architectural and other means. Older shopping complexes, including Delhi's Connaught Place, offered a degree of shop and street interface by being tropically porous realms (even allowing a little *paan* shop to flourish in the cracks). However, most new malls are hermetically sealed interiorised enclaves that are in complete visual and attitudinal denial of their surroundings. The city is held at arms' length through a series of barriers, by the visually resplendent architecture, by the curtailing of interaction with the surrounding city, by the inevitable motorised access, and by the spectacular security befitting a royal precinct – all of which work towards intimidating groups that are not participants in this new urban experience. The residential enclaves are also similarly policed and truncated off the continuum of the city. The metrosexual citizen can now travel from home to mall, bypassing the rest of India.

The new mix is a double-edged phenomenon. If mix and hybridity are operative mechanisms for the realm of mass consumption, the vast mass is still held at bay. While spectacular cinematic means offer virtual access to anyone to the above arc of desire, not limited to an educated elite, spaces in the city are being fabricated that are distinctively the prerogative of a privileged group. As the 'local' gets reconfigured by the quasi-mystical figure of the NRI (non-resident Indian) who is now an inevitable subject of the transnational filmic imagination, access to other groups in the community is severely curtailed. ∆

Notes
1 Homi Bhabha, *The Location of Culture*, Routledge (London and New York), 1994.
2 The term was derived after a conversation with Michael Meister.
3 Brian McHale uses Thomas Pynchon's *Vineland* to understand the Postmodern ontology of television. 'Much in the same way ... that [Fredric] Jameson has sought to convert the spaces of postmodernist architecture into a tool for thinking about ("cognitively mapping") the otherwise elusively unrepresentable system, Pynchon may be seeking to convert TV into a tool for cognitively mapping the place of death in a postmodern culture. And much as Jameson has strangely, and controversially, redeemed even so unlikely a building as John Portman's egregious Bonaventure Hotel by appropriating it in this way to his (and our) cognitive use, so Pynchon has, perhaps more strangely still, "redeemed" TV.' Brian McHale, *Constructing Postmodernism*, Routledge (London), 1992, p 141.
4 Fredric Jameson, *Postmodernism, or the Cultural Logic of Late Capitalism*, Duke University Press (Durham), 1993.

TWENTY-FIRST CENTURY CHINA

The anonymous, characterless model of new high-rise urban housing juxtaposed against, and soon to replace, the existing, low-scale residential.

Setting foot in China in the mid-1970s felt like stepping back in time 50 years. Cars were few, trucks were basic and the horse and cart was commonplace. The most sought-after commodities were bicycles and black-and-white televisions. Architectural memories were of the icons of the past: the Forbidden City, the Marble Boat and the Great Wall. The overall sense was greyness, from the Russian buildings of the 1950s to the uniforms of the militia. Returning to China today is like stepping onto a boom-town movie set with a cast of 1.3 billion. Particularly in the large cities, one's visual sense is filled with images of the new and the modern, with architectural forms rivalling those in any other part of the world, and with fashions straight from Paris or Milan. Wherever one turns, one is confronted with the new juxtaposed against the old, the 19th and the 21st centuries. The seemingly surrealistic scene of a family tilling their plot of dirt, with a small, dilapidated hut as shelter and horse and cart as transportation, abutting the latest *faux* Mediterranean-style

American architect Edmund Ong describes the new China he encounters on his return after three decades. Struck by the pure alacrity of development, he is also startled by the extreme juxtapositions of old and new. He observes an unprecedented free-for-all environment that contends with many of the same urban dilemmas already encountered in 20th-century America.

gated community complete with mission tile roofs, lifted straight from a Las Vegas suburb, is not an uncommon sight in present-day China.

The most striking results, however, are in the large urban areas. When comparing Beijing and Shanghai with the cities of 25 years ago, what impresses is not only the magnitude of changes, but also the speed and pace with which such changes are occurring. An obvious question is how a country of 1.3 billion people can transform itself so rapidly from a 19th-century society into one of the potentially most powerful economies in the world.

A major factor is politics. Although differing from one country to another, politics is always an integral element of development. For American cities, decisions regarding new development often begin at the neighbourhood level. In China, major policies and directions are developed at, and come from, the top down. Evidence 1979 when Deng Xiaoping dramatically instigated a revolutionary change in direction in China by opening the country to the West, followed by a major reform to a socialist-oriented market

In the foreground, a neighbourhood with the urban clutter resulting from the accumulation of a century of organic growth, a future victim of the inexorable march of the skyscrapers, as seen in the background, representing the new China.

The old and the new. Overhead is the spaghetti of elevated freeways that is evidence of the contribution of American cities to the Chinese urban fabric. What this scene will become, as car ownership in China increases from the current 15 per cent in large urban areas to the 30 per cent common in Europe, or perhaps the 80 per cent of the US, is difficult to imagine. Parked underneath are bicycles – that ubiquitous form of ecologically sensitive private transportation of the masses, now considered obsolete in the minds of many public officials.

After the Deng Xiaoping endorsement of private ownership and a socialist-oriented market economy, the opening of China to development resembled a California gold rush.

The calm and serenity of the Forbidden City belies the physical and visual chaos of new development in Beijing.

economy. This centralised decision-making authority and the ability to make major decisions rapidly exists not only at the national, but also at the local, level of government.

Although generally appointed, Chinese mayors do share a common goal with their elected brethren in the rest of the world, and that is to succeed. An administration that demonstrates leadership and progress with concrete results often leads to a higher position. Prime examples of this in China are the previous mayors of Shanghai, Jiang Zemin (who became president of China) and Zhu Rongji (who became premier). So, inherent within the Chinese system is not only an ability to make decisions with a speed unknown to US politicians, but also an incentive to take full advantage of it. Combined with the ability to implement decisions, it becomes apparent why the country can modernise at such an incredible pace.

A friend, visiting China shortly after its opening, prepared a documentary titled *The Wild Wild East*. This may also, for the many developers and architects and planners, aptly describe their experiences of working in China. After the Deng Xiaoping endorsement of private ownership and a socialist-oriented market economy, the opening of China to development resembled a California gold rush. It seemed as if everyone, from experienced overseas developers to state-owned enterprises, whose *raisons d'être* were in other areas, but who controlled large resources, jumped into the development business.

In pursuit of the pot of gold, however, there also appears to be a desire on the part of many developers, public and private, to author projects that reflect the technological prowess of China and signify its importance in the world. In addition there is an apparent unacknowledged competitiveness among cities and developers, who vie with one another to develop attention-grabbing signature projects. For architects, this represents a once-in-a-lifetime opportunity to propose forms and designs that previously were only dreams. And this perception is reinforced when examining the commonly used design competition process in which teams with too little time or funds to carry out adequate analysis or produce thoughtful designs submit the most eye-catching proposal in the hope of being selected. The result in this free-for-all environment is, in many instances, an apparent pursuit of form as an end in itself, an interest in external form and image over substance.

The overlay to all of this is speed. For developers, time is money. As a result, they are forever imposing aggressive design schedules. But they usually are also experienced enough to understand what is realistic. However, indications are that many clients in China, new to the game, have unrealistic expectations about the time and effort required to accomplish a project. For the architect, this results in an inability to spend the time necessary to examine design alternatives in a comprehensive and cohesive manner, or to develop the competition-winning dream concept into a mature and developed piece of urban design or architecture.

The impression of Beijing 25 years ago was that of an orderly planned, axial city of megascaled blocks and gigantic avenues, befitting its status as the capital of China. Notwithstanding this, the city had a low-scale and fine-

An entire district of Shanghai with its plethora of architectural forms and materials is evidence of the lack of public control and a boom-town character where anything goes.

An example of the pressure to develop housing to meet an overwhelming demand, with the resultant lack of concern for the principles of good planning and sensitivity to developing a livable environment.

A reliance on the old rather than the new to activate the public realm.

Nanjing Road, Shanghai's historically famous shopping street, now turned into a pedestrian precinct.

A lively neighbourhood with the ever-present modern high-rise looming in the background.

grained character, defined by the ubiquitous *hu-tongs*, areas of single-storey residential units organised around a labyrinth of pedestrian-scaled streets and alleys circling the centrepiece of Beijing, the Forbidden City. Greater building heights could be found as one moved further out from the city centre.

Arriving in Beijing today, one is immediately struck by the bright lights and neon, not unlike any major international city, and the crowded streets and plethora of high-rise megaprojects, sprouting up everywhere in a seemingly random and incoherent pattern.

Looking across the river from the Bund in Shanghai 25 years ago, one could see an area consisting of agricultural and industrial uses. Today, it resembles a 21st-century Gotham City, with high-rises of differing forms and shapes and materials clashing with one another.

Much of the planning for new developments in China appears to be based on a superblock module, a possible remnant of the Russian planning of the 1950s and also a result of the need to accommodate and increase the speed of development. As American cities discovered, however, the superblock module appears to be more appropriately designed, in terms of scale, for the car rather than the pedestrian. The problem was further exacerbated when little attention was given to how these projects met the ground, how they related and contributed to the public realm and to the development of the connective tissue that links projects into a cohesive whole. Now, American cities and their planners have finally become more sensitive to the value-added benefits of developing projects that give

attention to the pedestrian experience and contribute to the activation and enhancement of the public realm, and to the importance of developing the linkages that create neighbourhoods. Unfortunately, many of the new mega-developments in China still possess, from a Western perspective, similar shortcomings – a series of singular trophy projects unrelated to one another.

For a large part of the 20th century, transport for most Chinese was either by foot, public transit of some type, or that most sought-after commodity, the bicycle. However, this is no longer the case. The motor car, that great symbol of mobility and, more importantly, of status and prosperity, has made tremendous inroads as the preferred means of transport. It has become, like the television a quarter of a century ago in China, not only an instrument of convenience, but also a symbol of success.

In Beijing and Shanghai, roads that 25 years ago were populated with bicycles are now gridlocked with cars. Six- to 10-lane thoroughfares cut through the hearts of these cities, causing great damage to the urban fabric and the pedestrian realm, as well as having an untoward consequence for the populace. Of all traffic-related fatalities, only between 3 per cent and 4 per cent are occupants in cars – the remainder are motorcyclists, bicyclists and pedestrians.

Approximately 78 per cent of the US population owns cars. In China this is close to 3 per cent, although about 15 per cent in Beijing and Shanghai. An unfortunate by-product of the increased mobility that the car brings, however, is enabling and reinforcing a horizontal development pattern. Twenty-five years ago, Beijing had one ring road, with proposals for a second. Today there are five ring roads with a sixth to be constructed in time for the Olympics. This urban sprawl is no different to what occurred in many American cities, prime examples being

The new Shanghai, a man-made forest of tall buildings stretching as far as the eye can see.

Los Angeles and Atlanta. Here, the focus was on the needs of the car with little thought given to the parallel development of a comprehensive public transport system. The result is terrible traffic congestion, pollution and quality of life issues. And as such cities are now discovering, the cost and disruption to retrofit a public transit system into the existing urban fabric is enormous.

Shanghai and Beijing are now facing these issues as they plan major expansions of their subway systems. Of greater concern, however, is that many other Chinese cities, now on the cusp of major development, are also focusing their attention on accommodating the car with much less thought for developing a comprehensive private and public transport system.

As the needs of the car remain foremost in the minds of many officials, there are now examples of bicycles, still the main mode of individual transportation for the majority of people, being banned from some of the newly built roadways. This thinking, as well as exacerbating problems of congestion and pollution, can also be seen as disenfranchising a large segment of the population who, for economic reasons, still rely on the bicycle.

For American cities, the issue was not to eliminate the car, but to develop a comprehensive private and public transport system that offered alternatives. Evidence indicates that not only is this less costly before major development occurs, but for China would begin to address the potential social problem of accommodating the multitudes who still will not be able to afford a car.

In China's rush to build big and build new, it is clear that minimal attention has been given to the old and the existing, although the speed with which development is occurring certainly has also minimised the opportunities for an informed dialogue regarding retention.

The skyline of the new Pudong area of Shanghai as viewed from across the river. Punctuating the line of high-rise buildings is the Pearl of the Orient Tower to the left, for many ordinary Chinese the symbol of the prowess and capability of the new China.

As a result, substantial sections of the existing fine-grained historic neighbourhoods that defined the urban fabric of Beijing have disappeared, and are continuing to do so. It is estimated that more than 60 per cent of the low-scale, fine-grained *hu-tongs* that defined the city fabric have been destroyed, with more scheduled to be demolished.

Although Shanghai also has seen demolition of much of its existing architecture, it would have been much worse if it had not decided to locate its new financial headquarters and central business district across the river in the Pudong area, which until 15 years ago was devoted to agricultural and industrial uses.

Despite all this, there is evidence of a developing sensitivity to the existing. There are examples in Beijing and Shanghai of a pioneering, grittier adaptive reuse of existing industrial warehouse type buildings that are being converted into artists' studios, art galleries and similar. Shanghai is home to arguably the highest-profile adaptive reuse project in China, the Xiantindei development, designed by Wood-Zapata. The development is in a part of the city where the French concession was located, and is also the site of the first Communist Party headquarters. Existing small-scale, two- and three-storey buildings were retained and sensitively reconstructed with pedestrian-oriented retail commercial premises including shops, restaurants and bars. Not only has it turned into one of *the* destination places in Shanghai, its success is motivating other cities in China to want to replicate it.

Hopefully, these projects are a first step towards a heightened awareness and discussion of the issue of retention. However, as American cities discovered, retention and restoration can be extremely expensive and, in many cases, impossible without incentives. For China the issue is further complicated by the

realities of the living conditions of the average Chinese. This said, one can understand an expressed preference on the part of many to live in a brand-new high-rise in an apartment that has more space, new appliances, heat and working plumbing. But the question of retention is more nuanced than either total preservation or total demolition. And in the process, we have also discovered the value of retention of the existing, as representative of the history and culture of a society.

What is apparent when looking at much of the planning and development in China are the similarities to that which occurred in the US. Decisions related to planning and development in Chinese cities mirror those made in American cities in the mid-20th century and that are now, with hindsight, looked upon ruefully. The superblock development pattern, the focus on accommodating the car to the detriment of public transit and the pedestrian, and the inattention given to the public realm, are all reminiscent of the urban planning and design that grew out of the Modernist movement of the 1920s and were implemented during the renewal of American cities in the 1950s and 1960s. What urban renewal did in American cities in the mid-20th century was, and is, being done in China 50 years later.

Although China is socially and culturally different to the US, an internal dialogue that focuses on the significant issues related to urban design and architecture that were faced by American cities is still important to determine their applicability to China as it continues to modernise. Concerns are being raised as to whether China and its cities, in the understandable rush to modernise and to capture the country's share of the developing global economy, will also end up destroying their past. This is significant if it is deemed important to retain vestiges of one's history. A related question is whether, in the

A typical new multitower high-density residential project in Shanghai, built adjacent to an existing development, clearly illustrates the dramatic changes taking place within the urban scale and fabric of the city.

information age of the 21st century, with globalisation and an apparent homogenising of world culture, it is important or even possible for cities to maintain an identity of their own. Or will Chinese cities that are being rebuilt, not incrementally, but almost totally over a short period of time, represent the first of a new paradigm – modern metropolises of the 21st century that are indistinguishable from one another or from any modern Western city?

Also becoming obvious is not only the quantity of natural resources that are being absorbed by China to fuel its reconstruction, but the repercussions of this on the rest of the world. Over the long term, it is clear that China, if it continues to expand at the present rate, must give serious attention to development of more environmentally sensitive strategies. Fortunately, there is evidence of this in a number of areas, from cleaner-burning energy sources to strategies related to green architecture and to the pursuit of energy-efficient cars.

The hope that these issues will be addressed rests with the new generation of architects and planners, many of whom are in their forties, were trained abroad and have returned to China to practise, as well as with the younger professionals who will be the next generation of decision-makers. Their exposure and travels to the West have, and will, allow them the opportunity to see with a more critical eye what has occurred in the renewal of American cities over the last 50 years, and will sensitise them to the problems of development and its relationship to the urban and social fabric of the society.

Many such professionals already realise that they represent the leading edge in examining these profound issues and investigating the validity of establishing a relationship between a contemporary architecture and a new Chinese culture and identity, as the country and its economy mature. They also realise that it is essential to develop strategies to deal with natural resources and energy, and that in the process they can demonstrate to the world China's creativity and technical prowess. What they discover and develop will shape the new China and in the process may well inform the West as to the role of architecture in shaping a society and culture. There is an old saying that 'I have seen the future' and, in this case, it is China. It will be fascinating to see how that future develops and what that future becomes. ◬

The rubble of the old makes way for the new.

The photography for this article is by Edward Denison, the photographer and co-writer (with Guang Yu Ren) of *Building Shanghai: The Story of China's Gateway*, which is to be published in early 2006 by Wiley-Academy.

HOLL ON HYBRIDS

Since his 1970s *Pamphlet Architecture* series on American architecture, Steven Holl has exhibited a unique ability to pinpoint intersections of culture and building. To gauge exactly how this current of thought might be running through Holl's present explorations, which range from small-scale domestic homespun projects to substantial schemes in China, guest-editor **Everardo Jefferson** interviews Holl at his New York base.

Linked Hybrid building complex, Beijing, China, 2003–
Upper-level bridges connect housing with shared functions such as cafés. The building's exoskeleton permits beam-free ceilings in all apartments.

One of the ongoing fascinations of Steven Holl's work is his ability to take the particulars of a given site, its history and its programme, and bring out their deep currents through a process of abstraction. The exploration unfolds with strong narrative and psychological undertones, resulting in designs of engaging strangeness. The process of mixing and hybridisation filtered through a gifted artist's mind.

A prime result of this process is Kiasma, the Finnish Museum of Contemporary Art, where the curving building section allows its 25 galleries to capture the horizontal light of Helsinki. The forms draw an implicit cultural line to Finlandia Hall, intertwining the building's mass with the geometry of the city and the natural landscape of Toolo Bay. Material attractions of the local building culture, such as the extensive use of copper on the outer walls, are generously encompassed within a work of art that embraces the present moment.

From the earliest projects, like the 1975–76 Manila housing proposal, Holl's work has manifested a fascination with the contradictions of order and individualisation, of local culture and abstraction. In his 1989–91 Fukuoka Housing, the local tradition of flexible sliding-door spaces is transposed into the hinged interiors of the 28 unique dwellings. Visceral images of black-wood-stave churches and sod roofs inform the characteristically layered concepts of the Knut Hamsun Museum project; conceiving of the Building as Body, battleground of invisible forces; in architectonic terms, aiming to concretise the essence of Hamsun, Norway's most inventive 20th-century writer.

With these images and ideas still haunting us, we wondered how Holl's present work might extend this wide vein of thought.

What Is Identity?

Holl's current projects range from exhibitions in Italy to an individual home in Essex, New York, to vast multifunction complexes in China. Given that, for Holl, a building's relationship to its site sets architecture apart as an art form, do cultures less familiar to him than that of the US effect an alteration in his design process? On the contrary, Holl directs the reader to his previous writings on site as the physical and metaphysical foundation for architecture: 'Especially when it's in a different culture, I use the principles I described in *Anchoring*, developing hybrids to create an identity unique to the circumstances of the project.'

How, then, can a foreign architect set about developing a project's identity in a culture like China? Holl regards the opening that has occurred for international design in China within a much wider historical context: 'Classical Chinese cities were places of deep symbolism. Then, in the mid-20th century we have the functional city of Mao. Now we are in a moment of new possibilities, of combining the most technologically advanced systems, green urban systems and layered cultural programming into a new hybrid – dynamic and porous.

'China at present is undeniably globally connected, supported by a global commerce. The cultural part of the new Chinese city should not be a kitschy re-creation of tradition, but a place of new symbols. The question is, then, where do you start?'

Manila Housing, The Philippines, 1975–6
To create a livable context for squatter settlements, the initial construction builds the 'absolute minimum proposal': definition of public/private line, permanent tenure and utilities.

Fukuoka Housing, Fukuoka, Japan, 1991
Interiors of the apartments revolve around 'hinged space'. Diurnal hinging allows an expansion of the living area during the day, reclaimed for bedrooms at night. And episodic hinging reflects the change in a family over time, adding or subtracting rooms.

Knut Hamsun Museum, Hamaray, Norway, 1994
Sod roof and black wood are pierced by hidden impulses – 'empty violin case' balcony and 'girl with sleeves rolled up polishing yellow panes'.

'Our Chinese projects embrace cultural connections and modern technologies to look to the next urban topologies'

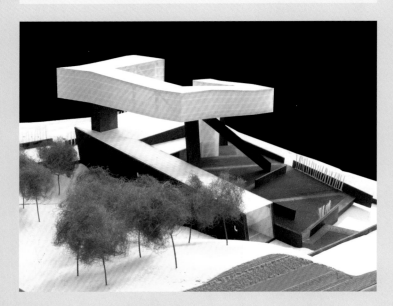

China International Practical Exhibition of Architecture, Nanjing, China, 2003–
Aerial view: the museum is formed by a 'field' of parallel perspective spaces, a method of shifting viewpoints derived from Chinese landscape paintings.

The interest in architecture as a promulgator of symbols drives both architects and their clients. The American late-19th-century Shingle Style is an example of a period in which clients were hiring architects to furnish them with an identity of class and 'tradition'. Image-givers like Stanford White and Bruce Price created large mansions, clad in brown shingles, with exquisitely proportioned wood details and expansive flowing spaces, to provide their *nouveau riche* clients with instant graciousness and a visceral visual link to the dark-wood homes of New England's puritan founders.

Later, New York's Museum of Modern Art (MoMA) of the 1950s provided Americans with a powerful sense of corporate identity, creating a series of museum shows that canonised 'good' design, creating an identifiable look to be used for 'progressive' urban headquarters, suburban homes and, even, product design.

So, at this pivotal moment, at the start of the 21st century, what does Holl believe identity means to his clients, especially in dynamically evolving China?

Holl replies that the China International Practical Exhibition of Architecture in Nanjing started with identity: 'Our Chinese projects embrace cultural connections and modern technologies to look to the next urban topologies. In the apartments of our Linked Hybrid building complex in Beijing, we followed feng shui principles by using an exoskeleton to create large areas of flat slabs to eliminate all overhead beams in people's homes. One of the "green" aspects of the project is that all 800 apartments connect to the greywater basin that creates the central space within the complex. Located within this central space are cultural facilities like the cinematheque. The upper-level bridges also connect the buildings with functions such as cafés. So the project brings together green building techniques and cultural spaces – a 21st-century identity warmly embraced by today's China.'

Culture as Architectural Language

What might the formal result be of this engagement with identity and specific cultures? How might culture translate directly into architectural language, most specifically, say, in the use of colour and materials?

'We use colour sparingly, but in locations that are noticeable. Colour is used on the underside of bridges, on soffits, in the microsection between inner and outer surfaces. To select the actual colours I took a Tibetan temple's official colours, making a chart in abstraction, and used the *I Ching* to operate a random process of selection.'

So do culturally sensitive relationships drive the creative process? Holl reflects: 'I make cultural relationships but I reinvent them. I create links back. An example is the Nail Collector's House, a 950-square-foot house for Alan Wardle in Essex, New York. The house is on the site of an old nail factory. The owner wanted a "poetic utterance" related to the site. The sheathing is cartridge brass; there is a sinister 19th-century aspect, nails exposed, which is related to the history of the site. The shape of the building is also related to the history of the site, to the verticality of the buildings in that town. The space spirals upwards in hanging platforms, culminating in a pinched "prow" towards the lake. The cost of this house is only $280,000. Clearly, when we're talking

'Consistency of language is commercially successful, but I'm doing the opposite – a new expression for each site, a love of small houses. For me, invention must occur at all scales of building'

Nail Collector's House, Essex, New York, 2005
The building shape is reflective of the verticality of surrounding structures. The pinched prow of the house inflects towards the lake.

Linked Hybrid building complex, Beijing, China, 2003–
A greywater lake provides the setting for these cultural buildings. Colours derived from a Tibetan temple are used on the underside of bridges, on soffits, and in the microsection between inner and outer surfaces.

Green Urban Laboratory, Nanning, China, 2002
Town plan preserving the two existing hills. In the foreground,
low-scale housing aims for porosity with natural ventilation and shading.
Green roofs are hydroponic gardens accessible to residents.

**Porosity Overlap, Cosmit's 'Entrez lentement' exhibit, Salone
Internazionale del Mobile, Milan, Italy, 2005**
Below and right: Experiments with Alba Flex material, using different
patterns and degrees of porosity.

Shadow Screen, Cosmit's 'Entrez lentement' exhibit, Salone Internazionale del Mobile, Milan, Italy, 2005
Alba Flex used as porous cladding.

Conference Room Door, Steven Holl Architects, New York, 2000
An example of ongoing materials research: a hinged panel deriving from an aluminium insulation product.

about these issues, money is not the point – for me, invention must occur at all scales of building.

'My approach is not a commercially viable activity for a lucrative practice. Consistency of language is commercially successful, but I'm doing the opposite – a new expression for each site, a love of small houses.'

This dedication to research as it relates to the making of buildings, from vast to small, leads to the natural question of whether materials research is part of the exploration process. How does Holl transpose materials to new uses and means of fabrication?

'I'm always doing materials research. One example is the door to this conference room. It originates from an aluminium insulation product – we asked why not use it to make door panels? Alas, the production cost to start making doors would drive up its price to about $800 per door, not a sellable figure. I did this in 2000; five years later foamed aluminium has become more economical.

'Another example of our research is on the wall, exploring using digitally driven perforating technologies to create exhibit panels, testing porosity for an exhibit in Milan. We will use a new material called Alba Flex. About a third of our projects were consciously selected to learn something. Many of our projects began with weeks of research on the site and the history of the region.'

Can the client be influential as an artistic agent in the exploratory process? What does Holl get from his clients?

'I get a partner in the creative process. You can't do creative architecture without the 50 per cent collaboration of the client. To me, this is not something to be ignored. A collaborator is someone to be enjoyed. I'm not an obedient architect, but the joy is when the client starts to get excited and involved. An example of a great client is Charles Price, the owner of the Stretto House. He was raised in a Frank Lloyd Wright house – as an eight-year-old he cut the opening ceremony ribbon for Frank Lloyd Wright's Bartlesville Oklahoma Tower. He grew up as an ideal client.'

Given that so many factors combine, especially if architecture is to be culturally sensitive, how can this result in a formal approach?

'Every site and every situation has the seed of its own formal language. I'm doing the opposite of those who design with a consistent formal language in all situations. Unique materiality and form bring meaning to the situation. Today, it's an open case for architecture. We can do anything. So with invention the site can establish its own meaning.'

But does Holl actually see it as providing content?

'Content is very slippery isn't it? Making something that gives an optimistic dimension of the place is a basic aim. Meaning grows with the myth and the time. Duchamp's urinal had less meaning when it was made than it has now, with all the thoughts that have accrued to it.'

Thoughts accruing to architecture – an architecture that is expansive enough to contain histories and futures specific to its rooted location; this is a goal that is demanding of a constantly directed search for embedded spirits and new meanings. To borrow an analogy from Holl, we think of his design methodology as sponge-like: with enough consistency of approach to provide structure for enquiry, yet porous enough to allow for the infiltration of new experience. Δ

AUSTRAL

Does a notion of unfolding Modernism, enriched by
cultural mix, stand up in contemporary Australia?
to the quick and questions Modernism's relevance
itinerant condition.

ASIA

a broadening of the
Leon van Schaik cuts
for the antipodean

It is not evident to me that Modernism has ever been an available strategy to Australians, living – as they perceive themselves to live – on an extreme periphery of the world. Certainly the classical universalising certainty of modernity that peaked in the 1920s in what was even then not a singularity – as evidenced in the bruising contest between Le Corbusier's grand vision of architecture as servant to the state, any state, and Meier's '*existenzminimum*' social architecture – was not available. There were direct and unruffled translations from Le Corbusier into the totalitarian regimes of Brazil and South Africa, but no such direct flow into the more democratic antipodes. Australian architecture was cushioned by its direct connections to London, through which flourished a vigorous subaltern arm of Arts and Crafts.

A few works directly derived from English Modernism (for example, the Tahara Road apartments in Cairo) did arrive. There was a fascination with Aalto's Finnish Pavilion at the World's Fair – an almost instinctive grasping at this work from another of the world's peripheries. Modernism as mediated into a style by the Museum of Modern Art's 'this is modern architecture' did eventually arrive,[1] post-Second World War, through Boyd's reworkings of the 1930s US domestic Modernism documented by MoMA. A succeeding generation embraced the Case Study houses, and this is a recurring source of inspiration in those cities that have yet to establish their own architectural discourse.

But the Australian mindset seems to have always been in a second-order relationship to Modernism, warily observing itself trying on the style, taking liberties with the canon justified by an ironic embracing of the tyrannies of distance – as exemplified in Howard Raggatt's (of Ashton Raggatt McDougall/ARM architects) recollection[2] that in the textbook available to him as a student the photograph of the Villa Savoye was printed back to front. All diasporas take on a mantle of multiple identities – something that critics, from what they themselves regard as the metropolitan cores of Modernism, find very difficult to comprehend. And Australia has been suspended between its mother country, its largely suppressed Aboriginal heritage, its halting embrace of the New World[3] and waves of migration that have added Italian, Greek, Maltese, Dutch, Lebanese, Chinese, Vietnamese, Chilean, Argentinean, Sudanese, Iraqi and others to a largely UK-derived settler population. The UK is still the source of most migrants.

So does the notion of an unfolding Modernism, enriched by a broadening of the mix, make any sense here? Or is this notion of a 'new mix' another attempt to assert the hegemony of the one right path of Modernism that Critical Regionalism heralded in the 1960s? On that occasion, regional climate was allowed to 'enrich'. What emerges in the diasporic cultures is irredeemably plural and second order: architectures and self-aware irony. Every Australian architect is both here and somewhere else – as indeed in some essential way is everyone on earth, but in the antipodes this is a front-of-mind condition. There are mutually conflicting clusters of agreement about where that somewhere else should be. There are those who see this somewhere else as the indigenous past and either combine European mythology with an interpretation of

Sean Godsell, Carter Tucker House, Breamlea, Victoria, 2000
The Carter Tucker House sits in the lee of an ocean dune, facing north to the sun. It unfolds to the outside on three sides, with a circulation spine across its southern face.

indigenous lore, as does Greg Burgess, much of whose practice has concerned interpretive centres for sacred sites; or incorporate into their design the innate and tragic conflict between sacred knowledge that retains its value only if it is passed from initiate to initiate and the modern notion of transparency, as does the Terroir practice when working in similar terrain.

This is treacherous ground, with an ancient knowledge system seemingly devoid of any but a starkly instrumental architectural tradition luring architects, settler and Aboriginal alike, into embracing Postmodern formalism as an expression of what that tradition might be beyond the utilitarian. In this context, the sleight of hand that in the 1960s linked bark 'humpies' to the Barcelona Pavilion and begat Murcutt's *oeuvre* seems to be about appropriation pure and simple. The overtly political work of ARM's National Museum points to a new, perhaps less patronising way of addressing these issues, even if the result, in the short term, has been merely the arousing of neo-conservative ire. Time will tell. ARM's strategy on the Melbourne shrine, in which the firm works from the settler heartland towards an inclusion of others seems to offer a more enduring and 'hearts and minds' winning approach.

That settler heartland is itself conflicted with desire. Nicholas Murray, a young architect working mainly in multimedia installation with a profound concern for the impact of soundscapes on our sense of being, devises in 'Birds and Bees' what seems to be a cosy doll's house, but rumblings from low-resonance sound sources disconcert anyone entering. Murray works to simulate the actual discomfort that everyone subliminally feels about their tenuous reaching from the primal sexual and territorial urges from which we try to win relationships and the higher-order meaning systems of art, music and architecture. This is a mix that Modernism has suppressed in its Faustian compact with objective reason, a compact that has twice brought forth the monsters of world war, and in the continuing Proto-Modernist denial that our primitive being maintains our world in an unending recursion of violence. Murray and his collaborators seem refreshingly willing to confront experience in all of its layers, not only the rational. As I have previously

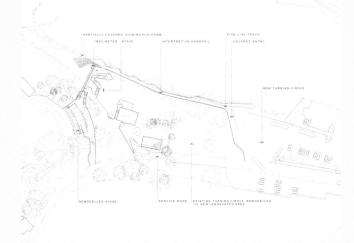

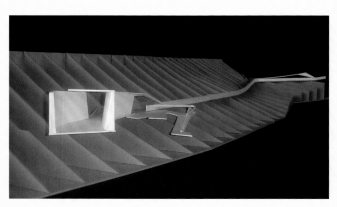

Terroir, Viewing Place, Cataract Gorge, Launceston, Tasmania, 2005–
The 1:500 concept plan shows how the architects are forming an arrival route that delivers the visitor to the central pool of the gorge in a scenographic simulacrum of the existing route from its mouth. The model shows how the architecture frames this up, referring only analogously to what can be shared about the traditional knowledge of the site.

Greg Burgess, Uluru-Kata Tjuta Aboriginal Cultural Centre, Yulara, Northern Territory, 1995
This design subtly evokes the tradition of care for the environment that is at the core of the 40,000 years of Aboriginal civilisation in Australia. The plan was evolved in a participative process with the local traditional owners of these sites, known to settlers as the 'Red centre'.

described,[4] this includes using light with sound. In the Birds and the Bees, the scale of the doll's house confounds, but it also brings symbols into play. From a distance the surfaces seem covered in innocuous and now commonplace Laura Ashley wallpaper. However, up close, the wallpaper seems to be a field of bees, and one discovers that each motif is composed of sexual symbols – breasts, bums and penises. The savage and the civil ride in close tandem, and even though the work is – as is always the case with Murray – genial in feel, it flips us in and out of safety.

Sean Godsell, also from that settler heartland and now internationally recognised as a leading Modernist, follows in his father's avowedly Modernist quest. But he has found inspiration in the ascetic refinements of Kyoto temples, and reached through that to peers of regional architecture like Swiss architect Peter Zumthor, rather than to any of the current Modernist mainstream. There is something of a Zen sensibility in the very fit between Godsell's increasingly ethereal cages of space and their sites – a fit that is so perfected that these buildings do not look new. The Carter Tucker House is a box on a dune that unfolds to become inhabitable, the walls becoming screens that filter the sun. One can imagine the house in time-lapse photography, through a 24-hour cycle and through the seasons, almost as responsive to its situation as is the turning head of the sunflower to the sun. The Mornington Peninsula House, on the other hand, is a cage of laths around a glass box that seems to have been discovered embedded in a fold in the land. It has such a sense of rightness that it seems as ancient and as inevitable in its landscape as the temples of Kyoto are in theirs; temples that paradoxically may well be in construction terms – depending on the maintenance cycle – quite as new as Godsell's houses. It is just as difficult to label Godsell as a Modernist as it is to use the term to say something meaningful about Zumthor, whose St Benedict chapel at Somvix replaced a chapel destroyed in an

Nicholas Murray, Melissa Bright, Shelley Freeman, Jono Podborsek and Kirsten Grant, The Birds and The Bees installation, curated by Hannah Mathews in spare room@project space, Royal Melbourne Institute of Technology, 2003
Left to right: the entrance to the doll's house, the 'birds and bees' wallpaper motif and the interior of the doll's house.

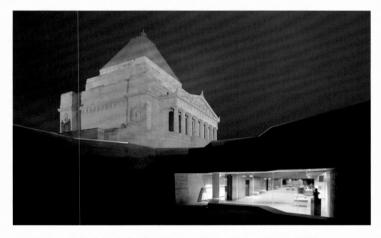

Ashton Raggatt McDougall (ARM), Melbourne Shrine Visitors Centre, 2004
ARM has undercut the shrine with fractally derived incisions, providing informal access under the ceremonial axis. In this way the settler/empire tradition is maintained, but the complex is opened to new readings by citizens from different backgrounds.

ARM, National Museum of Australia, Canberra, 2003
While the skin of the building and its plan comment on the past, a Boolean stream penetrates the building, setting up a dialogue with the more multicultural present, and thus embracing the future optimistically.

Sean Godsell, Peninsula House, Mornington Peninsula, Victoria, 2002
Also in a dune system, the Peninsula House is barely visible until one drops down into it along its east face, arriving in the living area that opens out to a barbecue deck.

Daniël Cleemput, House Cerkez (above), Carlton, Melbourne, and Owen Studio (below), Collingwood, Melbourne, both 1999
These buildings for artists introduce a new notion of *architectura povera* to Melbourne, one that exposes a rationalism that is in powerful contrast to the slick Neomodernist style that pervades much less considered design in Australia.

avalanche and, in responding to this, has – as do Godsell's works – an engineered quality though lacking any of the ubiquity of engineering solutions. It lacks also the remorseless ubiquity of the style that we know as Neomodernism.

Migrant to Melbourne Daniël Cleemput has added his own Belgian minimalist sensibility to the mix with a series of *architectura povera* works of stunning technical simplicity. These houses for artists are possible because the clients are themselves intrigued by novel propositions, have limited budgets and have often found – as Nikos Papastergiadis has shown artists do[5] – possibilities for inhabitable sites that no-one else has seen. These subtly altered warehouses (like that for the sculptor Robert Owen) and constructions on slices of seemingly too narrow land (like the house for artist Mutlu Cerkez), are serenely rational, but arise from interactions with clients who are engaged in challenging the orthodoxies of Modernism.

Asian influences are difficult to discern despite the growing presence of people of Vietnamese and Chinese origin. As in my observations about Nicholas Murray and the ways in which we win our civility from the teeth of our primitive selves, there does seem to be a hierarchy of concerns in settlement, which initially skew the professions in favour of surveying, engineering and law – so that land could be parcelled, accessed and traded[6] – with design emerging only as a much later concern. This seems to play out for each wave of settlers, with the professions of preference for first-generation offspring being medicine and law. Asian influence is more evident in intercity relationships. For example, Australia has an architectural kinship with the diaspora state of Singapore, with which it shares a language, a flight path to Europe, and a common colonial history.

Kerry Hill, an Australian architect based in Singapore, has reinvented an Asian vernacular in a series of resorts that have reawakened the tropical sensibility of a region that had come to equate comfort with air-conditioned enclosure behind Modernist glass. From his office has emerged a school of 'lush situation' architecture trained to ensure that every head that hits a pillow in a resort has the same privileged view across lawns to a pool and the beach beyond. Leaders in this are WOHA designs, one of whose principals, Richard Hassell, is – like Hill – an Australian from Perth. Australian-educated architects work across the entire Southeast Asian region. Many, like Australian-educated Singaporean Look Boon Gee, make a distinctive contribution to the emergence of sustainable local cultures of architectural innovation.

Hong Kong had a period in which Australian architects made a major contribution, with the Hong Kong Club, a seminal design by Seidler, originating the city's enduring preference for Modernist design. Recent Australian influence has been more baleful, with a strange obsession in Hong Kong for outdoing the Sydney Opera House, an obsession that has not produced one work of note. These two-way flows are worth watching. China is awash with schemes designed by Australians in one of the biggest carpetbagger booms in architectural history. Whether anything of enduring interest emerges seems unlikely to me, holding as I do that architecture at its best emerges

Kerry Hill, Apartment Building, Bangkok, 2005
The reinvention of an Asian tropical architecture by Kerry Hill continues in this new apartment building in Bangkok.

Look Boon Gee, Bishan Community Library Project, Singapore, 2005–
This community library is designed to present as much of its workings to the outside world as is possible, a desire for readability that characterises the diaspora.

Ivan Rijavec, Alessio House (exterior) and Freeland House (interior), Melbourne, 1997 and 1994.
Like many people who have experienced more than one continent, Rijavec is fascinated by perception. These houses use cambered walls and ceilings to create environments that alert visitors to their spatial perception mechanisms.

Richard Hassell/WOHA, Alila Villas, Pecatur, Bali, approved for construction 2005
View of terrace. The 'lush situation' that WOHA engineers in all its projects stems from the firm's deep involvement in the design of tropical resorts, initially during the architects' time in Kerry Hill's office.

from, and contributes to, local cultures. There are those who settle in a city long enough to become part of its culture, as Lab Architecture did while designing Federation Square, but their major work is now in China. Perhaps here, too, as in Singapore, it is Australians, like James Brearly, who began to seek work in the booming city of Shanghai, then married into and migrated to the city, who will make a contribution that will resonate eventually back in the architectural culture of their country of origin.

Back in Australia, relative newcomers have made major contributions. Nonda Katsalidis, born to the Greek diaspora that has made Melbourne the third largest Greek city, has done much to transform citizens' ideas of what it is like to live in the city, leading a wave of well-designed inner-city apartment blocks, many named with a migrant sense of the politics of the future – Republic Towers (named during the failed referendum seeking to separate Australia from the British Crown) and Eureka Towers (named for an early uprising of miners fighting for their rights against the colonial state). Katsalidis brings a thoroughly Mediterranean sensuousness into his work, a quality sometimes referred to as 'boomstyle', and one that certainly distances his best work from Neomodern ascetics. Eli Gianini and Nicholas Goia are in conscious dialogue with their origins in Italy. Ivan Rijavec has worked from an almost 'cabinet of Doctor Caligari' mental space towards a much less chiaroscuro position, but one in which space is always worked energetically and unexpectedly. Another notable local innovator, with a fascination for the relationship between real and virtual space, is Slovenian-born Tom Kovac. He is one of the few Australians who play into the architectural forums of nonstandard architecture – a movement that Frederic Migayrou has identified as suppressed by Modernism's drive to conform to the standardising systems of the industrialisation of the 19th and 20th centuries.

And there is another wave of invisible migrants, English speakers from southern Africa, whose influence has been infrastructurally notable in Perth and Melbourne, seeking perhaps to redeem through subtler orderings the control societies they have left behind? Patrick de Villiers has been instrumental in saving Fremantle from destruction by traffic engineering and unmediated commercial expansion (only to have this undone by the dead hand of a university that is buying up the individual properties that are the glory of the city, and neutralising them by turning a major section of the city into a single-use entity).

Rob Adams, of Zimbabwean origin, educated at the University of Cape Town, has made a major contribution to the reinstatement and extension of the underlying principles of the urbanity of Melbourne, without which the city would have continued its headlong collapse into the nihilist Modernistic freefall that it embraced at the time of the 1956 Olympics. His work on maintaining and extending the lanes and boulevards of the city, and stopping developments that kill streets by turning their backs to them, has led the central city to reinvigorate itself. When he started this work as city urban designer, Melbourne was leaching activities to suburban centres at a rate that our research showed had reduced variety by 30 per cent in the decades since 1956.[7]

Where recently this infrastructural intelligence has been

QV Site, Melbourne
Top: Kerstin Thompson Architects, building housing crèche on top level, 2004.
Middle: Lyons Architects, BHP Billiton HQ, 2004.
Bottom: John Wardle Architects, QV Apartments, 2005.

combined with a design procurement process that I (also often reported as a South African migrant – though my architectural roots are more English than South African)[8] introduced to Melbourne in the late 1980s, works of enormous significance have emerged. Chief among these is the QV site in central Melbourne, which layers parking, regional scale supermarkets, food courts, laneways of fashion shops and coffee bars and restaurants, the headquarters building for BHP Billiton, a crèche, a corporate front office for Sensis, a layer of white goods and furniture retail, and housing over a system of laneways that links three levels to the streets surrounding the block. While the architects are almost all graduates of the Royal Melbourne Institute of Technology (RMIT) invitational Masters programme, not migrants, this complex brings to Australia for the first time the layering that characterises the new Asian urbanism.[9] This is a layering that Modernism abandoned except in Hong Kong, where the huge density of human occupation has always supported the many-layered city dreamed of in early modern thinking.

Something 'new mix' has certainly occurred in this complex, and in the nearby Melbourne Central, in which a Halperin-influenced retail maze and theme park super-block has been carved into by architects ARM, establishing lanes and connecting them to the surrounding lanes and streets, and opening up the perimeter walls to the streets with multiple tenancies on the scale of the old 19th-century fabric. The marriage of European urban principles laid down in the colonial period, and the inescapable experience of what our Asian neighbours are doing, has created a new urban form that combines the rationality of the grid city with the teeming population of space of the Asian city. It is no accident that this coming together of systems – understanding how to promote inner-urban activity, how to marshal patronage in support of local architectural culture, and a major presence of apartment dwellers, many of them students from Asian cities – has produced such a new urban form. The exuberance and diversity of the architectural expression reflects the maturity of one Australian city's architectural culture, one in which *techne*, poetics and civic narrative provide three poles to a vital discourse. ⌂

Notes
1 In 1932, HR Hitchcock brought European avant-garde architecture to the US 'New World' as a style rather than as an intellectual approach.
2 Leon van Schaik (ed), *Fin de Siecle and the Twenty-First Century: Architectures of Melbourne*, RMIT (Melbourne), p 120.
3 Paul Fox identifies a long struggle between those who sought to emulate the old country and those who embraced new ideas, agriculturally at least, from the New World of the US. Paul Fox, *Clearings: Six Colonial Gardens*, Melbourne University Press, 2004.
4 Leon Van Schaik, 'Wayfinder, Cate Consandine and Nicholas Murray at Connical, April 2003', ⌂ *Club Culture*, Vol 73, No 6, Nov/Dec 2003.
5 Nikos Papastergiadis, *Metaphor and Tension: On Collaboration and its Discontents*, Artspace (Sydney), 2004.
6 Brian J McLoughlin, *Shaping Melbourne's Future*, Cambridge University Press (Cambridge, Melbourne, New York), 1992.
7 Unpublished thesis by Kathy Greening, RMIT.
8 *Belle* magazine, No 152, April/May 1999, pp 30–48.
9 William SW Lim, *Asian New Urbanism*, Select Books (Singapore), 1998.

WEEKSVILLE
EDUCATION BUILDING

For award-winning New York practice Caples Jefferson Architects, the commission to design an interpretive centre for the Weeksville Society in Brooklyn offered a rare opportunity to explore African architectural form and to connect to the totality of the black experience in the borough. As guest-editor **Sara Caples** explains, it also required taking on board the input of a third party in the mix, representing the city's interests.

Cultural extensions are sometimes easily accepted as part of architectural projects. But, often, the discourse becomes more problematic – a source of friction on the way to creating its own mix. Caples Jefferson has recently experienced some of the contradictory pulls and conflicts of creating such a project.

The brief was to design a new interpretive centre and landscape extension for an African-American heritage site in Brooklyn. The project began in consultation with the site-based client, the Weeksville Society, as a series of explorations of Afrocentric form. However, once the results were presented to the citywide Art Commission charged with the aesthetic reviewing of all publicly funded projects, the project began to take a different turn.

Close-up of main entrance with shiplapped ipe wood and mottled purple slate in a scarification pattern.

Site History

After the end of slavery in New York in 1827, a group of freedmen led by James Weeks acquired land for homesteads in a less agriculturally productive area of rural Dutch Breuckelen. Located along an old Indian trail called Hunterfly Road, this unincorporated settlement later became known as Weeksville. Founding black churches, creating free schools for 'coloured' pupils, acting as a stop along the underground railway sheltering slaves fleeing from parts south, Weeksville was one of the few identifiably prospering 'African' communities of 19th-century New York. As the city became a centre of immigration and increasing urbanisation, by the end of the 19th century Weeksville had been gradually subsumed into the gridded blocks of the new homes of the German and Irish working-classes. It became all but forgotten until the 1960s when, with the rising importance of the civil rights movement, came renewed interest in African-American history.

Intrigued by 19th-century written accounts of the Weeksville community, an African-American historian and his urban-planning professor friend flew a helicopter over the historic area to establish whether any physical vestiges of the historic community remained. A cluster of houses strangely twisting off the street grid was spotted in the middle of an ageing tenement block. When the men visited the houses on the ground, not only did they discover buildings in an older farmhouse style: they also found descendants of some of the earlier African-American inhabitants still living in one of the homes. Amidst great excitement, the Weeksville Preservation Society was formed, and the history of the site patiently researched via archives and archaeological remains.

Forty years later, the houses are being restored as a heritage destination. The rest of the block to the east has been acquired and will eventually become an interpretive landscape, with an introductory and conference centre for visitors to the site.

Hunterfly Court: the rediscovered Weeksville houses in their 1960s condition.

The Cultural Brief

Our initial conversations with our client, the Weeksville Society, included their repeated direction to look back to the African roots of the Weeksville inhabitants for inspiration for the new educational building. At first, it was not clear to us why we needed to look any further back than the 19th-century farmsteads. However, gradually we realised that the new centre building should connect to the totality of the black experience in Brooklyn, to the revived 1960s interest in Afrocentricity as well as to the stories of the Weeksville ancestors.

African Prototypes

Although my partner and I had perused the occasional book on 'primitive' structures, we were essentially ignorant of most non-Western architecture. Fortunately, one of our colleagues at Caples Jefferson, Audrey Soodoo Raphael, has been studying African architecture and its African-American offshoots for at least 20 years. We soon determined to look only at areas of Africa that would have been home to those unfortunate souls snatched off to the slave pens. Even within a relatively confined area of central West Africa, the richness and range of building solutions was a revelation. Ingenious buildings ranged from the peanut-shaped Fulbe grass dwellings in Mali to the cliff villages of the Dogon people, to clustering villages of classical round-plan cone-roofed buildings.

We were especially struck by the earthen castles of the Joola people in southwestern Senegal. These circular compounds serve as refuges for the family, shelter for cattle and granaries for rice. Originally, these defensive enclosures developed to protect their extended family of 200-plus inhabitants from slave-trading raids. Concentric rings of storage, stable and dwelling surround central impluvia where water collects, people gather and grain is milled.[1] We were moved by the beauty of the funnelled light, the centrality of coming together under the great

The 19th-century Weeksville houses were rediscovered from a helicopter because they were off the street grid.

sloping eaves. We felt we had found a precedent that would inform the present.

Initial Design Logic

We decided to order the spaces of Weeksville so that each major space would offer a strong impression of rounded space pierced by single-source natural light. Each major space would be a variation on this spatial theme, with the intervening spaces of a more rectangular order.

The building was strung along the eastern border of the site, the interpretive landscape bracketed between the historic houses and the new centre. Because our clients and the local residents loved the long view of the rediscovered dwellings as seen from the newly cleared eastern plots, we cut a series of transparent spaces between each function cluster. Each glazed court connected the passing pedestrian to a prominent feature of the site: an oblique view of the houses along a reconstituted Hunterfly Road, a view of a new sculpture by Chakaia Booker and, at the main entrance, the framed frontal vista of the old homesteads.

The building was kept intentionally low to the ground to allow the historic structures to dominate. We introduced a giant swale into the interpretive landscape in order to restore a farmland roll to the site, and located the administrative offices and service spaces at the lower level, supplying the office workers with a dramatic view of the ancestors up the new slope.

Form Explorations

Our initial plan was to make all the drama of the rounded spaces internal to the building, with a straight wall along the street and a green roof in accordance with our LEED Gold (US 'green' certification) level of sustainability. We made a series of study models to test the possibilities of rounded forms, internalised, mildly expressed, with an idea of framing the skylights in a nonrectilinear spidery web. Our client encouraged us to be bolder in the street-side expression of the main spaces – to bring a more distinctive character to the fore. They were concerned about the severity of a long straight wall and wished to see more stepping of the forms.

The resulting design presents a series of forms, the rounded walls of the major spaces bowing out towards the street, their planed roofs stepping up from the smallest workshop group to the largest form, the community conference and performance centre. No longer positioned

Joola 'Castle' courtyard, Senegal. Light and air enter through the funnelled roof.

Long view of the Weeksville historic houses revealed to the surrounding streets.

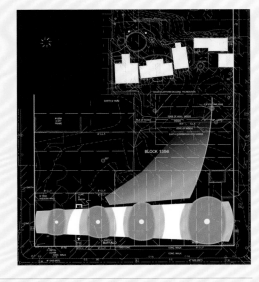

Initial-scheme diagram.

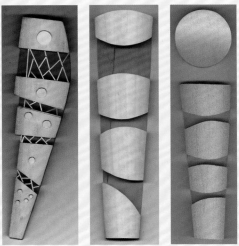

Early form studies alternating programme spaces and different degrees of transparency.

Early scheme. Building forms now pivot at transparent view slots to the historic houses.

Elevation along the street with wood-clad programme spaces and planted roofs.

View of the historic houses through the main lobby.

in a row, the building inflects at the two major transparencies, at the tour bus entrance along Hunterfly Road and at the main entrance, framing the view of the historic houses.

For reasons of both cost and aesthetics, the new educational building is clad in vertical clapboards made of iroko, an African wood. The power of this material is most strongly experienced in the dichotomy of the transparent slots, where the visitor is compressed between two tall sculptural round forms of dark wood, bridged by the more 'technological' steel and glass of the transparent roof and end walls.

Public Reaction

We were hopeful of a positive public reception. The project won a national design award from the National Organization of Minority Architects (NOMA) at about the time it was submitted to the New York City Art Commission for approval. After the initial presentation, most of the art commissioners went the extra step in visiting the site. They then called us in to share their concerns about the design.

The commissioners felt the new building presented too closed an appearance along the street, and wanted to see more openness. They were doubtful about the swale, about a building blocking the long view, despite our efforts at transparency, and were not at all convinced that the 'African' language did much to set up a dialogue with the historic houses.

Softening

We then submitted a redesign, retaining much of the earlier planning, but concentrating on a feeling of greater openness and accessibility. The circulation was flipped to street side and rendered transparent, a gallery for contemporary artefacts to be made by Weeksville's visitors, especially the local children, juxtaposing creations of the contemporary African-American community with views through to the forebears' abodes. The building's forms in this design wrap away from the street to draw the visitor gently around the block into the entrances. The retaining walls intersecting the swale were turned into gently planted slopes.

However, when the commissioners viewed the resubmission, they did not feel that it went to the heart of their objections. It was time to revisit the design anew.

Hardening

With our client's consent, we viewed the new design as an opportunity to revisit the language of the project, creating forms that were nonrepresentational, culturally nonaligned, yet with materials and details that would firmly express joy in African roots. To open up the street view of the historic houses, we sited two pavilions at the remotest corner of the site. The education and office pavilion provides direct views of the historic houses and acts as a generous portico, yet still provides a transparent view to the historic houses at the building's Hunterfly Road entrance. The large, fully transparent gathering space leads to a second pavilion that contains a changing exhibit-gallery, the conference centre and a resource centre for researchers.

The first redesign was similar to the early scheme but created more transparency within the building.

The final scheme moves rectilinear forms of the new building away from the view of the historic houses.

The revised final-scheme site plan replaces the swale with an evocation of farmscape in the main view corridor.

The final-scheme entrance elevation places a portico along the historic farm road.

In the final scheme, a wrought-iron fence with twisting pickets evokes planting patterns.

The site is more gently rolling, while our landscape architect, Elizabeth Kennedy, has introduced shaded groves and gridded agricultural plantings evocative of the homesteads' earlier surroundings. The building's upper floors are still of African wood, now the durable rich browns of ipe, while the stone base is of rough-hewn, mottled purple and green Vermont slate cut in patterns reminiscent of braiding and scarification.

The wrought-iron fence that surrounds the site is made of pickets patterned after African art. Each group of pickets twists in a different direction, creating an undulating three-dimensional enclosure. At first glance an almost normal park fence, but, on closer inspection, arranged to a more complex rhythm.

Hidden in Plain Sight

In speech, dress, music and literature, African-Americans are among the leading creatives in contemporary American culture. Yet, at Weeksville, there remained the issue of how to proclaim pride in the unfolding present without overwhelming the quiet history of the past. How to tone down the street dress of the new building without denying its origins.

Modernism as a style provides one such cloak – at its roots a style of architecture neutral in intent, clean of cultural encrustations and, now, in its third or fourth generation, reinvigorated with many stretched tendencies.

If one new mix was too alien for broad acceptance, Modernism offered alternative paths for hybridisation, combining more restrained forms with an overtly heritage-based materiality. Not hiding, but presenting a series of signals that allowed the ancestors' homes to remain dominant.

A language rich enough to allow stretching in a mix that brought all the city's communities into the dialogue. ᴆ

Note
1 For more of these moving images, see Jean-Paul Bourdier and Trinh T Minh-Ha, *Drawn From African Dwellings*, Indiana University Press, 1996.

Kazi K Ashraf teaches at the University of Hawaii's School of Architecture. He writes on phenomenological issues of architecture and landscape, and contemporary South Asia, and has recently completed a book entitled *The Last Hut: Dwelling in the Ascetic Imagination.* He also co-curated an exhibition on Louis Kahn's work in Dhaka at the University of Pennsylvania (2005) and the National Museum, Dhaka (2002), and was co-editor of *An Architecture of Independence: The Making of Modern South Asia* for the Architectural League of New York (1997).

Sara Caples and **Everardo Jefferson** are partners in Caples Jefferson Architects, a New York-based practice involved in public-sector and nonprofit work. Honours include local and national American Institute of Architects design awards, National Organization of Minority Architects national awards, and selection as Emerging Voices of the Architectural League. Their work has been featured at New York's Urban Center and at the American Museum of Natural History, and has appeared in numerous publications.

Teddy Cruz is an associate professor of public culture and urbanism in the Visual Arts Department at UCSD in San Diego, California. His work engages the border between San Diego and Tijuana, Mexico, searching to build an architectural practice, research and pedagogy from the sociopolitical and cultural particularities of this bicultural territory. His firm, Estudio teddy cruz, has been recognised in collaboration with community-based nonprofit organisations such as Casa Familiar for its work on housing and its relationship to an urban policy more inclusive of social and public programmes for the city. He has recently received the 2004–05 James Stirling Memorial Lecture on the City Prize.

Jamie Horwitz is an associate professor of architecture at Iowa State University, and has a PhD in environmental psychology. She teaches that cultural clashes are more than a visual phenomenon. Her study of MIT's Koch Biology Building was selected for the *2005 AIA Report on University Research*, and her chapter on design in the postdisaster community appears in *Sustainable Architectures: Cultures and Natures in Europe and North America* (Spon, 2004). The MIT Press published her co-edited collection *Eating Architecture* in 2004.

David Height is an architect with the project management section at Arup, before which he lived and worked in Tokyo. Having met Cengiz Bektas while studying Ottoman and Byzantine architecture at university, he spent a year in Kuzguncuk with the Bektas Studio, coming into contact with its artistic and literary community. Absorbing Istanbul, walking every district, and returning many times since, he still feels more familiar with its topography than with his native London. The experience led him to undertake further research on one of the city's historic quarters, and gave him the appetite for developing a deeper understanding of other urban cultures, ultimately leading to five years in Tokyo.

Iain Low convenes postgraduate programmes and research studies in architecture at the University of Cape Town, South Africa. He studied at the University of Cape Town and the University of Pennsylania, and was a Pew visiting scholar at the American Academy in Rome. His research area is space and transformation, and the post-apartheid condition.

Jeremy Melvin is a writer who specialises in architecture. He is a contributing editor to △, and has also contributed to many international architectural publications. He studied architecture and history of architecture at the Bartlett School of Architecture, UCL. He now teaches history of architecture at South Bank University, London, and is a consultant on the Royal Academy of Arts architecture programme. He is currently writing a book for Wiley-Academy on the contemporary country house.

Jayne Merkel is a New York-based contibuting editor to, and member of the editorial board of, △. She also writes for *Art in America, Architectural Record* and the *Architect's Newspaper*. Her most recent book, *Eero Saarinen*, was published by Phaidon Press in September 2005.

Edmund Ong is a graduate of the University of California at Berkeley. After working for Anshen and Allen, and then Joseph Esherick and Associates, he joined the San Francisco Redevelopment Agency. As its chief of architecture, he developed a design and development process and commissioned a range of work that has had a significant influence on the urban landscape of San Francisco. He has received a number of local and national citations for his work, including the AIA Thomas Jefferson Award for Public Architecture.

Ruth Palmon is an architect who is currently living in Tel Aviv, where she practises architecture and teaches at the David Azrieli School of Architecture, Tel Aviv University. She holds an MSc in architecture from MIT, and a BArch from the Bezalel Academy for the Arts in Jerusalem.

Leon van Schaik studied at the Architectural Association (AA) in London and is innovation professor of architecture at the Royal Melbourne Institute of Technology (RMIT). From his base in Melbourne, he has promoted local and international architectural culture through practice-based research. He is the author of *Mastery in Architecture: Becoming a Creative Innovator in Practice* (Wiley-Academy, 2005), and is currently writing a book entitled *Design City Melbourne*, which will be published in early 2006.

Anooradha Iyer Siddiqi, AIA, is a New York-based architect and the Robin Hood Foundation's Director of Library and External Initiatives. Her architectural practice includes design projects in the US and India, and investigative writing in the discipline. On a fellowship with the American Institute of Architects (AIA) and the American Architectural Foundation, she is currently researching relationships between urban geography and civic expression. △

98+   Interior Eye:
Turning Japanese
Craig Kellogg

102+   Building Profile:
**Senior Common Room Extension,
St John's College, Oxford**
Jeremy Melvin

107+   Practice Profile:
Hodgetts+Fung: The Art of Remix
Denise Bratton

115+   Home Run:
Westerton Road, Grangemouth
Henry McKeown

119+   Book Review:
Expressing More Than Structure
Kate and Ian Abley

122+   McLean's Nuggets:
Will McLean

124+   Site Lines:
Puerta of Dreams
Howard Watson

Interior Eye

MGM Mirage, Shibuya restaurant, Las Vegas, 2004
Behind the long, low sushi bar at this new Japanese restaurant by Canadian architecture firm Yabu Pushelberg, a video installation is diffused and diffracted through the sculptural wall treatment of mirrored plastic cubes.

TURNING
JAPANESE

Below
The designers specified wavy wood screens and grey tile
floors for semiprivate dining rooms at Shibuya.

Sin City looked East for inspiration and started getting real. Craig Kellogg stops for sushi in Las Vegas.

The writer Dave Hickey, a long-time resident, likes to say that Las Vegas was 'invented by the highway and the Mob'. So much for cultivating an old-fashioned creation myth. It wasn't necessary – or even necessarily advisable – to examine the details too closely in the 1970s, when Vegas glamour was only skin deep. Then again, the usual rules never really applied in this land of peach fuzz-flocked wallpaper and coldly sexual mirrored ceilings. Based on their Vegas research, architects Robert Venturi and Denise Scott Brown popularised the term 'decorated sheds' to describe the generic architectural shapes they found veneered inside and out with gaily flashing bulbs and tubes.

The city's megaresorts were jukeboxes themed around flimsy fantasies, from Excalibur to Oz. Smelling money, 'designers' arrived. With time, the boldly fake evolved into the coyly *faux*. The model then was Disneyland, and the overblown Styrofoam sphinxes started looking a little like sandstone. It was good enough if you kept the lights down low.

The city had once been an auto destination, drawing adults primarily from Los Angeles. Suddenly there were planeloads of visitors from all over the world – even families. Developer Steve Wynn was credited with bringing design to the Nevada desert for the newcomers. First he built the Mirage, and then the even better Bellagio before surrendering his empire to a rival. Today, the renamed company, MGM Mirage, is vying for

headlines with Wynn himself. His $1.83 billion Wynn Las Vegas resort debuted in April 2005.

Taking just one example from before the design revolution, the Japanese restaurants in old Vegas had milky plastic shoji screens and clumsily lashed bamboo. A lot of the diners were homesick Japanese tourists. In places like New York, Americans started turning to Japanese cuisine as an honest and healthy fresh alternative. In Vegas, the Asian influence (and expectation of quality) was a kind of antidote, says Sven Van Assche, the vice-president of design for MGM Mirage. Van Assche leads the effort to hire outside designers to create venues inside his company's giant windowless casinos, as 'part of a larger effort to transform the look and feel of our product', he says.

His department oversaw the creation of a Japanese restaurant that serves as an apt metaphor for the new Vegas. The place is called Shibuya, and it opened last summer in the MGM Grand Hotel and Casino. Shibuya is upscale, like a lot of the new Japanese restaurants. It is short on shojis. It certainly appeals to Japanese tourists, who find it bracingly modern, like something you might stumble upon in present-day Tokyo. But it also crosses over. To a British eye, it looks perhaps more modern than even anything in New York. Van

Crisscrossed pine strips and boxy pink pendants decorate Shibuya's hibachi bar.

Top
MGM **Mirage, Sensi restaurant, Bellagio Spa Tower, Las Vegas, 2004**
There's no hiding the kitchens at Sensi, a straightforward Las Vegas space by the
Japanese firm Super Potato. The giant slabs are natural stone.

Bottom
The monumental stone blocks continue into Sensi's dining room, which
is as restful as Shibuya is dramatic.

Crisscrossed pine strips are layered
against the illuminated walls in
Shibuya's hibachi bar. In the old Vegas,
plastic laminate surfacing was the
norm, but here the bar is black
marble. Shibuya's dining tables look
like rosewood – and designer John
Houshmand confirms that they are.
Houshmand is also responsible for
the host's podium at the entrance,
which was carved from a maple log.
Van Assche's rule of thumb for
materials: 'If someone can touch it,
it has to be real.'

Assche calls it a better product, for sophisticated
adults. 'We're turning a hundred this year, and it's about
time we grew up,' he says.

The Canadian design firm Yabu Pushelberg
introduced its own brand of showmanship, beginning
with Shibuya's etched-glass 'facade' that veils the front
of the restaurant. (Entirely interior space – and without
windows – the glass separates the restaurant from the
surrounding casino.) Straight ahead is a thick sushi-bar
top of cultured stone figured with jazzy veins, like a
granite slab on steroids. Chairs tucked underneath are
leather. The bar is backed with a 50-foot-long wall of
video screens behind a sculptural assemblage of
mirrored acrylic cubes. (So the kinetic light is diffracted
into abstraction.) 'At the end of the day, we're still trying
to entertain you,' Van Assche says.

Crisscrossed pine strips are layered against the
illuminated walls in Shibuya's hibachi bar. In the old
Vegas, plastic laminate surfacing was the norm, but
here the bar is black marble. Shibuya's dining tables
look like rosewood – and designer John Houshmand
confirms that they are. Houshmand is also responsible
for the host's podium at the entrance, which was carved
from a maple log. Van Assche's rule of thumb for
materials: 'If someone can touch it, it has to be real.'

The Japanese firm Super Potato applied this same
logic and specified giant granite blocks across the
street at Sensi, a new multi-ethnic restaurant in the
Bellagio's Spa Tower, which was completed last year.
'You could say we really went overboard with
respecting the materials,' Van Assche says. 'In the old
Vegas we would have faked it.' The visible kitchens at
the centre of a 10,000-square-foot space keep things
open and honest, as diners watch the chefs at work.
Down the street, at the Caesar's Palace casino, Dodd
Mitchell Design created Sushi Roku, a moody 315-seat
restaurant with pendant lighting fixtures of teak, bronze
and natural paper. Even further down the street, Wynn
has introduced – gasp! – natural illumination at Okada,
the Japanese restaurant at his new resort.

Designed by Hirsch Bedner Associates, Okada
overlooks a freshwater outdoor *koi* pond and 140-foot-
high mountain planted with mature trees plucked from
the golf course out back. If that seems just a little too
real (though the mountain is man-made), it no doubt
comes as a comfort that the old habits die hard in
Vegas. You just have to steer away from the
sophisticates and head to one of the city's older, mid-
priced properties. At TI, the former Treasure Island
hotel and casino, MGM Mirage has cheerfully reinvented
the free family-friendly live-action pirate show as a
skin-baring battle of the sexes. They don't call it Sin
City for nothing. **Δ**+

SENIOR COMMON ROOM EXTENSION,

ST JOHN'S COLLEGE, OXFORD

Top
A deep balustrade defines the edge of the lunch room some distance before the external glass wall, creating a two-storey void.

Bottom
Space is defined in several ways: movable shutters, a glass wall and the edge of various horizontal planes.

From the stone walls of St Giles in the centre of Oxford, St John's College presents a historic facade. Jeremy Melvin takes a tour of the college's quads and takes in some of its modern gems, the most recent of which is MacCormac Jamieson Prichard's senior common room – a space that demonstrates MJP's enduring 'capacity to surprise'.

Like many Oxford University colleges, St John's conceals its secrets well. A dull front quad guards the magnificent 17th-century Canterbury Court from the uninitiated, just as Tony Blair's presence among the alumni might dim its contribution to English literature through association with Kingsley Amis, Robert Graves and Philip Larkin. MacCormac Jamieson Prichard's Senior Common Room translates the same phenomenon to a contemporary construction project.

The extension lies behind various layers of concealment. A discreet passageway between the chapel and hall leads from the Front Quad, culminating in a sign with the deathless Oxonian inscription 'No Visitors Beyond This Point' just before entering the North Quad. Here is some recent architecture. ACP's Beehive Building of the 1960s is planned on a hexagonal module and its elegant detail gives it a more timeless quality than Arup Associates' temporarily influential Thomas White Building, the expressed muscularity of the construction of which now seems an archaeological survivor of those laboured 1970s debates about new building in historic

Top
View across the first-floor lunch room. When open, the shutters seem to draw the eye from the interior to the exterior.

Bottom left and right
Between the two giant portal frames is an unexpected rooflight. The outside walls are not the only source of daylight in the space.

Top left
First-floor new plan. The new lunch room nestles into its eclectic fabric, providing cover for 84 fellows, or can be reconfigured into a single large table for governing-body meetings.

Middle left
Ground-floor new plan.

Bottom left
Site plan. The senior common room occupies part of the North Quad.

Top right
First-floor previous plan. The suite of rooms has grown over more than 300 years.

Bottom right
Ground-floor previous plan.

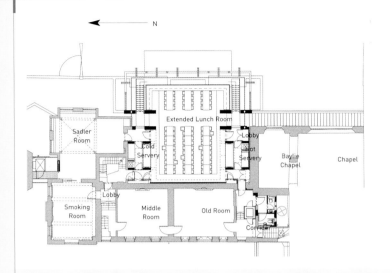

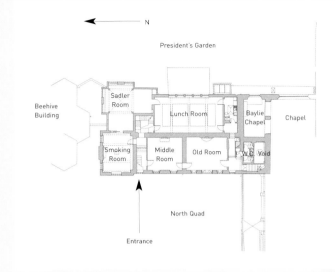

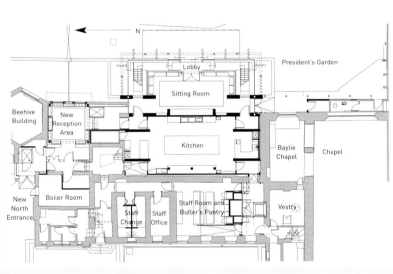

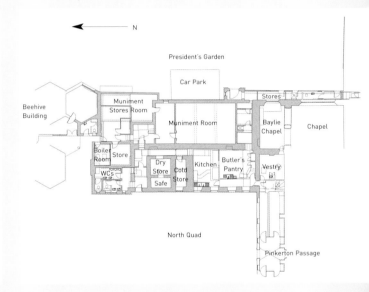

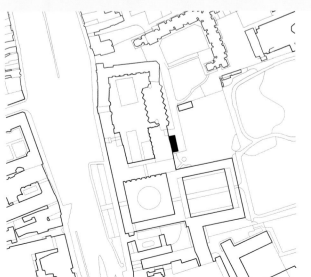

settings. Beyond this, MJP added the Garden Quad in the early 1990s, a subtly graded and richly composed residential building.

But back in the North Quad a late 17th-century facade, such as might be found in the better class of Cotswold parsonage, inscrutably conceals all manner of academic intrigue. Under 18th-century plaster or surrounded by early 19th-century decoration, in Edward Maufe's Arts and Crafts smoking room or the faintly Soanian Sadler Room, designed by college fellow and architectural historian Howard Colvin, generations of dons have drunk port, engaged in polite banter and decided the future of recalcitrant students. When, in the short interval between Garden Quad and the millennium, the college's fellowship grew to between 80 and 90, this motley arrangement of spaces no longer sufficed for the senior common room. Gentle accretion

105 +

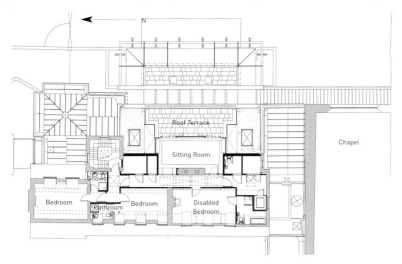

Second-floor proposed plan.

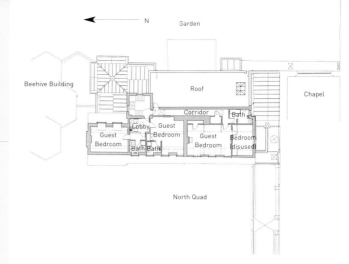

Second-floor existing plan.

and donly drawing boards were not up to the new demands. Something drastic was needed.

The historic surroundings are a good inoculation against the normal public-sector sense that design quality is an add-on luxury, but it still says much for the college's traditions and the perception of its fellowship that they selected MJP to design the extension. Though well known among Oxford colleges, and to St John's in particular since the Garden Quad, MacCormac's designs for them still have a capacity to surprise. The surprise stems from his personal reactions to the contingent particulars of brief and site, and the way he folds them into his eclectic range of architectural interests. Each project becomes an experimental vehicle for a certain agenda. Garden Quad, for instance, explored a range of ideas, including how a grand, formal composition could be approached through a modest gateway in a garden wall, which might be a loose metaphor for the informality with which Oxford sometimes cloaks its intellectual authority.

The senior common room investigates something quite different. Given the historic fabric against which it sits, there was an inevitable question about the relationship between old and new, which MJP's design turns into a deliberate surprise. But beyond this it also plays with that most elemental of architectural characteristics – space. The existing rooms in the suite gain their character through texture and decoration. The new rooms, and in particular the first-floor lunch room, are an essay in how volumes can be defined by invisible barriers and voids as much as by solid walls and planes.

In essence, the range facing the North Quad had little scope for alteration except for the kitchens and other ancillary spaces at ground level. But the newer additions, dating from the 1950s onwards and facing east overlooking the President's Garden, were less precious and offered scope for the necessary expansion. This was also a chance to tidy up the eastern end of the chapel, which abuts the senior common room to the south. The chapel had sprouted a lean-to that made an unliturgical incursion on the lower part of the east window. Its eastern wall provided one line that MJP marked with a large concrete portal frame. Another frame stands a metre or two further into the garden, and both provide almost all the main structural capacity. Beyond the second of these, the first-floor slab cantilevers with an outer row of timber piers that carry the shutters, gingerly landing in line with the edge of an existing path.

Typically, MacCormac cites numerous influences that swirl together, becoming explicit and fixed in the design rather than

in words. Two of these are particularly visible: the effect of Soane and especially the ambiguous definition of space and hidden light sources in his breakfast parlour at Lincoln's Inn Fields; and an ongoing fascination with the way Frank Lloyd Wright combined prospect with refuge. Refuge, in this club-like institution, is easy. Each of the existing rooms on the first floor is a comfortable refuge, and the first part of the lunch room, flanked by a pair of serveries and under a solid roof, suffers few immediate threats. But from it views extend outwards, through the pair of portal frames, across another run of tables, over a wide balustrade, across a void to the shutters which, if open, seem to direct movement into the garden. The tables beyond the portal frames are on the cantilevered slab, and although more visible, still have a sense of protection from the deep balustrade and the apparent *cordon sanitaire* of the void between it and the outer layer of glass. Of course, closing the shutters to prevent overheating from the easterly sun in the morning, or to avoid prying eyes during a governing-body meeting, could turn the whole space into a refuge. MacCormac's point is that it could be both refuge and prospect, simultaneously.

The Soane references are more subliminal. Between the portal frames is an unexpected rooflight, while the layering of spatial boundaries – from openable shutters to transparent yet unopenable glass – or voids, recalls but doesn't ape some of Soane's spatial tricks. The contrast here is with Colvin's dryly academic Sadler Room: it perhaps served as a vehicle for MacCormac's different level of homage to Soane, rather as Diabelli's simple waltz sparked Beethoven's eponymous *Variations*, or JS Bach's 'correcting' of Pergolesi's *Stabat Mater*.

It is in this territory, where influence is never certain and ideas might achieve temporary equilibrium, but are never fixed, that MacCormac thrives. Problem-solving is only part of the design process. There must be an infusion of cultural ideas as well. Oxbridge colleges may provide the raw materials for those cultural ideas, and receptive ground for their discussion, but that is a field of possibility rather than a predetermined path. MacCormac's importance to contemporary British architecture is that he can turn these possibilities into a design concept. ⚙+

American Cinemathèque at the Egyptian Theatre, Hollywood, 1995–9
Detail of the new acoustic panels lining the main theatre where they
abut the meticulously restored starburst ceiling.

Craig Hodgetts and Hsin-Ming Fung
are inspired by the 'diverse and
eclectic character' of their adopted
city of Los Angeles. As **Denise
Bratton** explains, LA seeps into the
very design process of their practice
as much as it informs the character
of their work. This is reflected in
their dynamic scenographic
approach, their bent for canny
improvisation, and their attention to
new materials and technologies.

HODGETTS+FUNG
THE ART OF THE REMIX

Top
Los Angeles Public Library, Hyde Park–Miriam Matthews Branch, 2004
The jig-sawed profile of the main facade adds a syncopated rhythm to the streetscape,
its roofline gleaming with copper cladding and a brightly coloured tile mural flanking
the main entrance.

Middle
The open and unhierarchic interior space is spanned by imposing
Paralam bents, and the ceiling plane is shot with strands of colour
interspersed with the gleam of irregularly positioned reflectors.

Bottom
Patrons working in the library glimpse punched-out shards of sky
through the latticework of the north facade.

Top
Los Angeles Public Library, Hyde Park–Miriam Matthews Branch, 2004
The jig-sawed profile of the main facade adds a syncopated rhythm to the streetscape,
its roofline gleaming with copper cladding and a brightly coloured tile mural flanking
the main entrance.

*We have built our design philosophy on the holistic
view that every aspect of our surroundings, from
tableware to thoroughfares, is a participant in the
human experience, and that the architect has a
right and an obligation to employ this arsenal of
experience in the creation of a compelling
environment. With the freedom to download and
remix, to morph from streetwise to strictly business,
our culture has staked out an age in which identity
is forged by the individual who assumes it. Why not
employ architecture as a catalyst, rather than a
constraint? Why not embed the behavioral cues, the
linguistics of posture, attitude, and action into the
fabric of our structures, rather than pursuing an
agenda of formal prescription? The diversity of our
work attempts to confront this challenge.*
— Hodgetts+Fung[1]

Though never for a moment losing sight of the essential
nature of the discipline of architecture, Craig Hodgetts
and Hsin-Ming Fung are bound and determined to
enlarge its boundaries. While their California-based
practice reaffirms architecture's commitment to the
principles of functionality and aesthetic interest, they
are quick to trade in the foundational notion of *firmitas*
or permanence, for flexibility and mutability, portability
and deployability, as the occasion presents itself.
Always seeking to evoke the theatrical dimension of
space and to anticipate the unequivocally analogue
nature of experience, Hodgetts+Fung are never satisfied
with mere phenomenological effects, instead deploying
the tactics of scenography to advance a critical position.

Hodgetts, with his industrial design expertise
grounded in Detroit-style assembly-line production, and
Fung harking from Southeast Asia, where nonstandard
uses of materials and technology bear witness to the
power of invention, share an affinity for making
something new and harmonious out of the most
disparate and seemingly incongruent materials and
technologies. They also share a finely tuned radar for
the subtle yet compelling elements of site and context
that inform their designs: 'Distant views, the pulse of
traffic, the immediacy of a historic artifact, and the
delight of the user's sensibilities all form a mosaic of
references and inspirations that give purpose to our
design. Like a system upgrade, these principles drive us
to strive for a nearly seamless intervention rather than
proclaim the birth of a new order.'[2]

The terms H+F use to describe what they are up to
speak volumes. In the spirit of the remix, their
buildings, projects and installations, as well as a
number of visionary works under way at the moment,
defy any claim to monumentality, instead valorising the
dynamic and ephemeral status of architecture.
Contravening traditional assumptions about the art of

building, their art of the remix invokes the metaphor of the operating system upgrade and the act of intervention, spelling out a canny position with respect to the challenges confronting architects in the 21st century.

Just months after the opening of their Hyde Park branch of the Los Angeles Public Library and the new Hollywood Bowl, and as they put the finishing touches on a monograph summing up their remarkably diverse body of work, H+F maintain a whirling-dervish pace. Their spacious Culver City studio is abuzz with work on their winning project for a performing arts complex in Menlo Park. While they shuttle back and forth between LA and Tokyo, where their Yamano school for aestheticians is under construction, they are conceptualising and designing a set of 'environments' for the new World of Ecology wing of the California Science Center in Los Angeles; developing a worthy follow-up to their acclaimed Blueprints for Modern Living and World of Charles and Ray Eames exhibitions, the Genius of Motion show for Art Center College of Design in Pasadena; fine-tuning a novel structural system for a block-long 'Big Top' to shelter next year's pre-Oscar rituals; and taking a moment to scout a historic 1920s Japanese movie house on Main Street in the old downtown core of Los Angeles.

H+F continue to conjure magic with their ingenious designs for libraries, buildings for the visual and performing arts, dwellings and spaces for leisure, exhibitions that become machines for learning, and others that project the scope of an entire era or field of design activity. Yet it is no illusion that their newest work seems only to deepen the eclectic range of patterns already etched in the practice they founded more than two decades ago. Each of their current projects partakes of ideas and solutions developed for projects dating back to the studio's beginnings (and in certain cases, its prehistory), some calling on concepts once considered unbuildable and even unfathomable, which have suddenly become viable as building conditions shift and market forces conspire to bring them into being.

To say that what they individually bring to the practice mirrors the diverse and eclectic character of Los Angeles – the city where they met and married and which they treat as a design laboratory – is not to short-change the extraordinary range of overlaps in their vision and orientation as architects and the consistent set of formal and technological trajectories their projects explore. Favouring industrial materials and applying their inimitable kit-of-parts sensibility, the partners combine the prefabricated and the custom-made with equal aplomb. Tilting towards the contingent and the temporary, they have long explored the parameters of tension structures – mobile components that give lift-off to Cedric Price's notion of 'anticipatory architecture'.

Hodgetts first studied engineering and automotive design at the General Motors Institute, a pioneering co-op school in Flint, Michigan, where he developed a formidable knack for drafting and a lasting fascination with the comprehensive nature of automotive design, in which the fine-tuning of every detail determines the success of the final product. At Oberlin College in Ohio, he fell under the spell of theatre arts, which led him away from writing and production work to the Actor's Workshop in San Francisco. In due course, he veered into architecture with the no-nonsense reasoning that he could 'make a living' drafting, only to discover that architecture was the right match for the scope of his diverse interests.

After graduating from Yale, Hodgetts gained much from the brief period he spent working in James Stirling and Arthur Baker's office in New York. He eventually took over their office space and launched Studio Works (1968–83) with Lester Walker, Robert Mangurian and graphic designer Keith Godard. Tenets were laid down in a series of inspired early works before Hodgetts moved to California in 1969 to take up the post of associate dean of the school of design at the California Institute of the Arts (CalArts). Under the auspices of the offshoot Works West, and in collaboration with Godard, Eugene Kupper and Peter de Bretteville, Hodgetts dedicated himself to a vision of architecture that gave its stamp to the deployable Mobile Theatre project that won them a First Design Award from *Progressive Architecture (PA)* magazine. Around the same time, Hodgetts invited Ant Farm to bring its Media Van to CalArts. These two events signalled the ascendance of a design culture devoted to mobility, technology and media in service of the unfettered dispersion of ideas and information, and a more profound experience of place – obsessions that Thomas L Friedman would recognise as early impulses of today's flat world.

Born in Hanoi to Chinese parents, Ming Fung moved with her family to Saigon before she was a year old. Growing up at the intersection of Chinese, Indonesian, French and American cultures, it was her father's world of film-making that seemed most compelling and attracted her to stagecraft. Ming's decision to become an architect led her to UCLA, where she met Craig Hodgetts; subsequent peregrinations to Paris, Hong Kong and Taiwan only drew her back to the celluloid city where the future is perpetually reinvented. When Ming returned to LA and invited Hodgetts to join her in a competition in 1984, the die was cast. With their sixth sense for spotting the essence of place and teasing new meaning out of existing conditions, H+F have adapted the processes and by-products of the region's aerospace and automotive industries as well as movie/media magic to generate a body of work that breaks down not so much along typological lines as on conceptual and morphological grounds.

An early, and as it turns out, pivotal influence was a series of collaborations with visionary director Robert Abel soon after the studio was founded. Convinced that computers were the future of visual effects, Abel

Top
Temporary Powell (Towell) Library, University of California, Los Angeles 1991–92
Conceived as an ensemble of tension structures deployed to temporarily replace the undergraduate library during an earthquake retrofit, the Towell's skeleton of regularly spaced aluminium ribs was covered with a stretched-fibreglass membrane anchored with laced cables to surrounding masonry walls.

Middle
Detail of the set designed for Wang Computers commercial, 1985
Pioneering the use of computers for special effects, director Robert Abel visualised

'connectivity' and the 'virtual office' *avant la lettre* by 'flying' images of H+F's minature sets around real actors in virtual space.

Bottom
Set designed for Cadillac Eldorado commercial, 1985
Striving to achieve credible presence for a toy Eldorado standing in for an actual car being filmed in the wide-open desert, H+F's miniature city was part of a huge 'supporting environment' that occupied nearly 12,000 square feet.

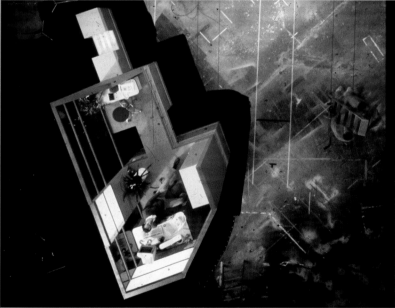

proposed to bridge the gap between analogue effects and early computer technology in a string of experiments including three commercial spots created with Hodgetts+Fung. Particularly memorable was a vast urban environment they created for the fleeting moment when a heroic Coke can would arrive in its fitted case, denuded of regulatory language, premium offers and bar code.

In this case, from the camera's point of view, H+F's meticulously realistic sets became mere background, each frame being all about that Coke can – not the architecture.

This and other early lessons about space, perception, focus and the supporting role of architecture have only been reinforced by H+F's projects for commercial buildings embedded in the harum-scarum urban fabric of LA. 'Observing cities and buildings, we find it impossible to separate foreground from background, building from context, architecture from urban artifact.'[3] H+F's most recent built work, two new branches of the Los Angeles Public Library system, indeed take their cues from the streetscape. After the conflagrations of 1992 following the Rodney King incident, which cost LA a number of libraries of no compelling character, the need for such places seemed to increase in the most blighted neighbourhoods of the city.

H+F's Temporary Powell, or 'Towell' Library on the Westwood campus of UCLA had already earned them a good deal of 'street cred'. The library's stunning economy of means and powerful presence made it a highly original work, albeit one conceived with a fixed life span. Like the androids in Ridley Scott's *Blade Runner* (and manifesting Cedric Price's dictum that a building should only last as long as it is useful), its expiration date was known at its inception. All the more was it missed when it no longer graced the patch of grass between the men's gymnasium and the dance building. With the Towell, H+F proved their ability to expeditiously meet the complex needs of librarians and students, and to build into the equation an elegant, if casual rapport with site and the sensual appeal of translucent and colour-soaked interior spaces. Their ability to distill the campus context to a few prominent scenographic elements that could be fed back into the design gave H+F the edge in the LA Public Library commissioning process.

However, their genius for temporarily integrating a brightly coloured 'inflatable' into the eclectic architectural context of the campus and making it seem at home was sorely tested in Hyde Park and Sylmar, two very different older neighbourhoods, both afflicted by depressed economies. This time the challenge was to strike the right note with new buildings for downtrodden streetscapes. In both cases,

the context was dominated by one- and two-storey bric-a-brac shop fronts, many with hand-painted signage fronting dingy sidewalks unmediated by the landscaping of better-off neighbourhoods. The other side of the City of Los Angeles' agenda was the cultivation of a civic sensibility for Sylmar, a mostly Hispanic community, and Hyde Park, an African-American enclave that saw some of the worst strife in 1992. H+F factored into the mix their own sense of the neighbourhood as place, relying for the rest on the input of residents who gathered for town-hall-style meetings. Testing their mettle as architects from outside the community on the proving ground of projects for crucial (and rare) public facilities, they arrived at an approach that met approval in each case.

The results have been telling. One could say that both libraries have completed their sites rather than overwhelming them, and have become centres of gravity rather than targets for vandalism. At Sylmar, the long, narrow building clad in corrugated shipping-container siding sits on a busy north–south thoroughfare running up into the foothills. This elevation is organised by a vector that runs from outside, where the building backs up to its parking lot, straight through the soaring glazed atrium to the intimate storytelling 'pavilion' at the front end where Polk Street meets Glenoaks Boulevard. From the all-purpose room towards the rear, fitted with state-of-the-art projection and lighting to accommodate community meetings, through the atrium, past vitrines, the circulation desk, stacks and seating areas, polished cement flooring and linoleum draw the interior spaces together as inside and outside are interlocked.

Drawing natural light as well as the hues of the sky and surrounding mountain views into the optic of patrons and staff, surrounding clerestory windows lighten the impact of the structure, while on the exterior, segments of the subtly canted roofline pick up the faded candy colours of mom and pop stores along Polk. At high noon, as the sun beats down and foot traffic peters out, the atmosphere of a ghost town from a corny Western is bolstered by dusky, drought-resistant trees and grasses that soften the edges of the street bordering the library.

The Hyde Park–Miriam Matthews branch is already treated with more respect by its users than anyone dared hope. Cutting a bold profile on Florence Avenue, the library earned local reverence through a participatory design process ensuring that this would not be just another intervention on the part of the city. Grounded in the language and palette of African art adopted by Modern artists in the 1920s and 1930s (but tinged with the 'bling bling' aesthetic of hip hop culture), the library functions as a gathering place as well as a refuge for readers and researchers, coming alive during storytelling and discussion groups. Drawing upon their commitment to the art of installation, H+F fitted the library with a high-tech display system that facilitates small exhibitions of objects and books that stimulate curiosity and spur further investigation. The whole speaks of a neighbourhood moving in a new direction. In fact, there is no need to 'tag' this building in order to claim it, as it belonged to the people of Hyde Park from the outset.

H+F's new performing arts centre for Menlo Park will take its place among their designs for 'show buildings', most prominent among them the masterful remix of the historic Egyptian Theatre on Hollywood Boulevard, which became the home of the American Cinemathèque in 1999, and their new Hollywood Bowl, which opened last summer to a plethora of commentary on its acoustic merit. Charged with transforming historic structures to accommodate new parameters and scales of entertainment, and thus the latest technology, H+F's schemes for the Egyptian and the Bowl cannot be adequately described as restoration or retrofit, conservation or preservation – yet all of these

Top
Hollywood Bowl, 1999–2004
The 'halo' that hovers beneath the curving arch of the newly-engineered shell is at once in repose and charged with geometric tension, hanging motionless above the audience.

Bottom
00:00, A Mobile Theatre, Prototype, Studio Works, California, 1972
Originally designed for the musical *Hair*, the deployable structure was to be installed in parks and playgrounds across the US. It was conceived as a set of reinforced fabric tubes inflated by semi-trailers containing high-pressure blowers, its double-membrane skin providing acoustical and climate control.

operations were involved. While respecting the historic identity and image of both buildings, H+F sought to reconceive the structures with the imagination and abandon that characterises remixing in the field of contemporary music. Apart from their sheer technical ingenuity and daring, in a city where tabula rasa conditions have indulged unchecked growth, and historic buildings have been routinely torn down and turned into parking lots, these two projects established a new standard for approaching historic theatres – many of which miraculously survived the 20th century, but may not survive the next decade of mega development.

Bringing their entire arsenal of architectural, technological and scenographic resources to bear, H+F upgraded every aspect of the Egyptian's functioning – projection, sound, seating, mechanical systems and circulation – to contemporary standards, while the historic interior decoration, marquee and monumental forecourt were meticulously restored to their original appearance. By reducing the seating in the main theatre, they were able to add a structural armature capable of supporting a new balcony, which was deftly inserted along with a more intimate, state-of-the-art black-box projection room installed below ground in a move recalling the form of a pharaoh's tomb.

Likewise, H+F's scheme for the Hollywood Bowl was conceived to work the old magic while quietly hiding a multitude of new tricks. Their charge was to optimise the Bowl's performance without sacrificing the image established in Hollywood's early years. The crux of their project was the invention of an acoustic device in which largely unseen mechanisms would provide an unprecedented level of sonic control. Conceptually akin to surviving descriptions of Brunelleschi's 'marvellous machinery' for the church of San Felice in Piazza in Florence, the 60- x 90-foot aluminium and fibreglass ellipse spanned by folding translucent panels forms a 'halo' that functions as an adjustable reflecting surface for dispersing sound among the performers and enabling them to achieve musical balance. Like the vanished Florentine prototype, it doubles as a suspended platform on which musicians can be positioned above the stage for dramatic effect.

Designed to permit a nearly infinite range of adjustments using a simple touchscreen, the panels lie almost flat during acoustical instrumental performances. Adjusting them for amplified or electronic performances is a matter of 'folding' them into a vertical configuration. Inclined about 10 degrees above horizontal to embrace the geometry of the Myron Hunt-designed natural amphitheatre, the halo optically engages the crest of seating, so that from a performer's point of view the relationship to the audience of 18,000 is more intimate. Against the backdrop of the lush Hollywood hills, the new, larger shell gives no hint of the radically remixed technology within.

One of the newest projects in the studio, in a class all of its own, is a deployable structure that will be unveiled just hours before the envelopes are opened at the 77th Academy Awards ceremony in March 2006 – and in the blink of an eye will be

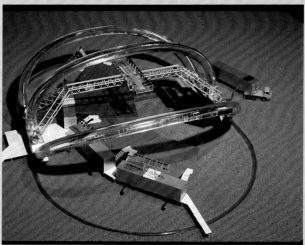

gone again. H+F's Oscars 'Bubble' spanning 400 feet of Hollywood Boulevard between Highland and La Brea is designed to shelter the pre-Oscar proceedings from the weather and ensure the comfort of Hollywood stars. The perennial 'red carpet' ceremony has become a hotly contested battle of sponsors and image-makers, in which intensified 'star' security after 9/11 is equalled only by the academy's desire to 'secure' logos and commercial sponsors' identities. In 2006, whole swathes of shop windows on the boulevard will be shrouded (a look anticipated over four decades ago by Christo's Four Store Fronts Corner) to prevent an errant brand from

Top
Model for Center for the Performing Arts, Menlo Park-Atherton High School, May 2005
Remixing a set of ideas that run through H+F's projects, some elements of the design seem to grow out of the ground, rising to meet other elements that rest lightly upon it like a hovercraft coming in for landing

Bottom
Oscars 'Bubble' project for the 77th Academy Awards, Hollywood, 2006
Countdown study for the installation of this novel deployable structure, in which a pair of high-pressure beams, held in place by a series of arches, tension the skin of the huge 'velum'.

peeking out at viewers around the globe. H+F's solution involves a novel structural system conceived for Studio Works' early Mobile Theatre project, which was impossible to fabricate at the time. The logistics are draconian: the city can only shut down the street for 36 hours to accommodate the assembly, and the whole thing must disappear before street sweepers come through.

With their new scheme for Menlo Park, H+F took a masterful approach to the landscape, radically altering the ground plane and orienting the theatre complex not to the street, but rather towards a venerable grove of oaks. A decisive move to depress the site by several feet functions to reduce the mass of the main theatre's fly loft, while beams rise up to embrace the multilevel complex, literally wrapping a sunken court for outdoor performances at one end. At the top of a great

stairway, the two-storey glazed atrium rises over an art gallery and ticket office tucked below, while a loggia running most of the building's length surveys the campus towards the south. Walls are surrendered to roof planes that fold down to enclose spaces and mediate between inside and outside, with glazing introduced to span the voids between. Drawing upon lines of investigation they have pursued over the past two decades, while promising to open a new era for the practice, H+F's performing arts centre for Menlo Park proposes a seamless intervention in the landscape that in turn becomes the rationale for the building itself. ∆+

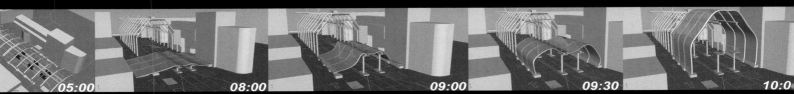

05:00   08:00   09:00   09:30   10:0

Notes
1 Craig Hodgetts and Hsin-Ming Fung, 'Introduction', in *The Art of Being There,* China Architecture and Building Press (Beijing), forthcoming, p 14.
2 Ibid, p 13.
3 Ibid, p 12.

Denise Bratton is an architectural historian, editor and publishing consultant, a member of the editorial board of ∆, and a protagonist for the journal *Log.*

Resumé

HODGETTS+FUNG

CULVER CITY, CALIFORNIA
FOUNDED 1984

CURRENT PROJECTS

- Wildebeest Music Pavilion, California Institute of the Arts (CalArts), Valencia, California
- Center for the Performing Arts, Menlo Park-Atherton High School, Menlo Park, California
- Yamano Gakuen mixed-use high-rise complex, Tokyo
- World of Ecology wing, California Science Center, Los Angeles
- Genius of Motion exhibition, Art Center College of Design, Pasadena, California
- Oscars 'Bubble' for the 77th Academy Awards, Hollywood, California
- Virtual House, Sagaponac, Southampton, New York
- Marlay House, Los Angeles

BUILT WORKS

2004	Los Angeles Public Library, Hyde Park–Miriam Matthews branch
2004	Hollywood Bowl, Hollywood
2003	Gershwin Gallery at the Walt Disney Concert Hall, Los Angeles
2003	Los Angeles Public Library, Sylmar branch
2002	World Savings and Loan Bank, Alhambra, California
2001	Sinclaire Pavilion, Art Center College of Design, Pasadena
1999	The American Cinemathèque at the Egyptian Theatre, Hollywood
1998	Disney Quest, Chicago, Illinois, and Orlando, Florida
1997	Mullin Sculpture Studio, Occidental College, Los Angeles
1995	Craft and Folk Art Museum, Los Angeles
1994	American Institute of Graphic Arts (AIGA) Gallery, New York
1993	Panasonic Pavilion, Universal City, California
1992	Temporary Powell (Towell) Library, University of California, Los Angeles
1992	Click & Flick Agency, West Hollywood, California
1990	Viso House, Hollywood
1990	Hemdale Film Corporation office complex, Los Angeles
1988	Goetz House, Studio City, California
1985	Corman House, Brentwood, California

INVITED COMPETITIONS

2005	Performing Arts Center, Menlo Park-Atherton High School, First Award
2003	Parque de la Gavia, Madrid, Spain
2002	The California Endowment Headquarters, Los Angeles
2002	Tempe Performing Arts Center, Tempe, Arizona
2000	Brooklyn Park Amphitheater, Minneapolis, Minnesota
1995	Expansion plan for Universal Amphitheater, Universal City, California
1994	Mobilized Assistance Shelter for the Homeless, Crisis Intervention Center, Las Vegas
1994	Vesey Place, Battery Park, New York City
1989	Arts Park, Los Angeles (First Award)
1988	Franklin/La Brea Housing, Los Angeles
1987	West Hollywood Civic Center (Award of Merit)
1985	Seoul Olympic Village (Excellent Entry)
1984	Urban Design Competition, Little Tokyo, Los Angeles (First Award)

INSTALLATION DESIGNS

1998	Fabrications, San Francisco Museum of Modern Art
1998	ZKT Wave Power, Elektrizitätswerk Minden-Ravensberg (EMR) Energie Forum-Innovation, Bad Oeynhausen, Germany
1997	Microsoft Pavilion, Electronic Entertainment Expo (E3), Los Angeles
1996	Microsoft Pavilion, E3, Los Angeles
1995	La Città Pulpa, Milan Triennale
1995	ZKT Sun Power, EMR Energie Forum-Innovation, Bad Oeynhausen, Germany
1992	Five Shrines, World Financial Center, New York

EXHIBITION DESIGNS

2000	The Science of Illusion, California Science Center, Los Angeles
1999	Memorias del Porvenir, Buenos Aires, Argentina
1997	California State Archives Museum, Permanent Exhibition, Sacramento
1996	Art and Film, The Museum of Contemporary Art, Los Angeles; Wexner Center, Columbus, Ohio
1994–2000	The World of Charles and Ray Eames, Library of Congress, Washington DC; Vitra Design Museum, Weil-am-Rhein, Germany; Los Angeles County Museum of Art
1994	The Magic of Play, Giorgio, Los Angeles and New York City
1993	Wings of Change, Giorgio and Director's Guild of America, Los Angeles
1990	Blueprints for Modern Living: History and Legacy of the Case Study Houses, Temporary Contemporary, The Museum of Contemporary Art, Los Angeles

PROPOSED HOUSING, WESTERTON ROAD, GRANGEMOUTH
LORETTO HOUSING ASSOCIATION LTD.

WESTERTON ROAD

GRANGEMOUTH

Henry McKeown looks at a social-housing scheme that Page + Park Architects has recently completed at Grangemouth, just outside Edinburgh. Below an exterior that exudes quasi-rural charm, McKeown reveals the necessary 'self-effacing honesty and endeavour deployed to make good domestic spaces and a good place to live'.

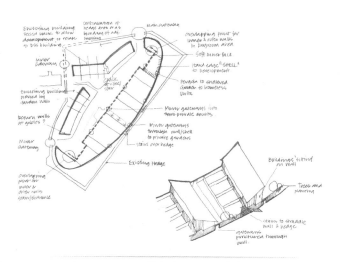

ENCLOSURE

WESTERTON ROAD	G 0-29%	F 30-39%	E 40%	D 41-49%	C 50-59%	B 60-69%	A 70-100%
QUALITATIVE							
Space-Interior					C		
Space-Exterior					C		
Location				D			
Community						B	
QUANTITATIVE							
Construction Cost						B	
Cost-rental/purchase						B	
Cost in use					C		
Sustainability					C		
AESTHETICS							
Good Design?						B	
Appeal					C		
Innovative?					C		

This table is based on an analytical method of success in contributing to a solution to housing need. The
criteria are: Quality of life – does the project maintain or improve good basic standards? Quantitative factors –
has the budget achieved the best it can? Aesthetics – does the building work visually?

Page + Park Architects has a long-established reputation
in Scotland for making good housing projects. Whatever
one may think of this work aesthetically, it is always
founded on strong conceptual ideas, usually relevant to
context, programme and clientele. For the architects,
housing is about a relationship between inside and
outside; interior space of a quality that invests housing
with meaning and raises the quality of life of the
residents. The clear definition of private and public
space through design is crucial to the success of
communal housing. Page + Park has created a clear
agenda to design the 'space between' buildings, ensuring
that this space will have a quality and a spatial meaning.

The project is located in Grangemouth, which is a
compact quasi-urban centre with a working port, major
BP petrochemical plant and an important transport
interchange. However, it is nonetheless a provincial
town, and this is reflected in the density of the
Westerton Road project, which has 52 housing units to
the hectare (156 bed spaces per hectare), arranged in
eight separate blocks, seven of which are two-storey
and one three-storey. The immediate housing context is
bland, but commercially could be described as stable
with a reasonable market demand for private and
rented accommodation. The existing urban fabric is
typical of many sprawling suburban edges – a mix of
four-storey council housing and two-storey semi-
detached housing, adjacent to light industrial and
community buildings. In townscape terms, this area is
unremarkable with few, if any, iconic buildings.

An underlying level of complexity and a range of
difficulties affected the Westerton Road project, most of
them disguised by its quasi-rural charm and apparent
architectural modesty. What should the site response be?
Take on the petrochemical plant or design against it?
Extend the existing fabric even though it is mediocre?
Address the park and hedge or simply create an inwardly
organised self-contained entity? Alongside this is the idea
of designing supported housing, resettling
disenfranchised people back into the mainstream
community, which in itself is a potentially tricky issue.
What implications will this have on the architecture?
Peel back the skin and one begins to discover the self-
effacing honesty and endeavour deployed to make good
domestic spaces and a good place to live.

The project rejects the current architectural
convention of falling into line with the new modern
methodology of making facade, and instead adapts a
sound, meaningful stance in designing housing from the
inside spaces out, and designing place (the space in
between) in an inventive and contextual way. This
architecture is not strident, but rich in its understanding
of the priorities that make social housing successful.

Neither project architect Alistair King, nor Simon
Carr, Director of the Loretto Housing Association, the

Top left
Grangemouth sits in the Forth Valley within commuting distance of Edinburgh.

Top right
View of street canopy over wheelchair unit.

Middle
Project viewed from the park.

Bottom
Montage of elements/forms (southwest).

GRANGEMOUTH

Proposed housing, Westerton Road, Grangemouth
Loretto Housing Association Ltd

Inchyra Park

client, can disguise their focus on and commitment to making good homes and good places to live. These are simple, yet critical goals where the emphasis is on people, families and their built environment.

Loretto is a fairly large housing association that provides housing to rent. What sets it apart is its mission to provide supported housing within mainstream housing accommodation, and it provides this in a fully integrated, seamless way. All of Loretto's projects are characterised by the social mix they provide. This means that they fully integrate and provide support for people all over Scotland who have been institutionalised in one way or another for most of their lives. This transition has been an overwhelming success, and has largely been credited to the high quality of the architecture the housing association demands. Carr is adamant that despite the individual personal circumstances within which people find themselves, we all respond in a positive, sensory way to well-designed, bright, interesting spaces. He also maintains that people are happier when their built environment is designed so that they feel secure and safe, and where their personal space offers them choices.

This is a highly commendable approach to designing housing, with the emphasis placed on the spatial quality of the interior and its relationship to the space beyond. It is less to do with architectural statement-making, but, rather, more concerned with prioritising the needs of the occupants.

The project succeeds in achieving the desired integration.

There is no hint of institution; there is no physical clue that this is anything but a very agreeable place to live, even though there is a support team on site as well as a dedicated common room, primarily aimed at tenants requiring support yet not exclusively theirs.

According to the Page + Park project description: 'The elliptical form gives the grouping a strong identity that encompasses variants of colour, materials and orientation, as well as a variety of plan types and resultant fenestration.' What the architects maintain is that the fenestration is not derived from a preconceived architectural language, but as a direct function of the plan organisation and juxtaposition of building blocks. This variation was encouraged by the client, who was keen to see a differing character to the individual houses within a unified form. The housing is accommodated within two-storey monopitched terraced blocks with metal (zinc and copper) roofs and timber (cedar) or rendered (full-strength colours from the Sto range) wall finishes. The form has been successful to the extent that many of the residents refer to the development as a village and strongly identify their house with its colour. This is an interesting observation since in discussion, Page + Park often referred to the strong formal arrangements of the coastal fishing towns of Fife and Aberdeenshire.

The client and architects have together created a unique self-contained architectural housing entity within which an otherwise controversial social mix is working in a nonobtrusive dignified way, where people openly and warmly tell you how much they love their homes, and where they feel secure and safe.

'The construction method was timber-frame superstructure on a reinforced concrete raft. The lightweight structure was a requirement of the poor ground conditions, but also permitted high levels of insulation and speed of construction. The client favoured a partnering approach to the construction phase and a site start was achieved in March 2000 following a negotiated savings exercise with the selected main contractor. The total construction cost was £3.1 million.'

The urban form creates a sense of enclosure and demarcates the outer shell of the public edge of the project. Within the ellipse, eight blocks are deployed to create a variety of subspaces. A crescent-shaped street (terrace form), two curved holding blocks make up the ends of the crescent – one a huge family house, the other the common room and support staff areas – and four stunted terraces form five small but delightful courtyards, bounded by a wall and the beech hedge facing the park. The ensemble works well and delivers a range of overlapping perspectives through spaces and existing buildings, making for a strong sense of townscape.

The key special characteristic of the housing typology is the through-plan that offers semi-open-plan space, from the front to the back of each house. Fenestration is modest; living areas are usually planned to take up the width between party walls and are substantial in proportion. However, the external outcome is less successful, with the solid to void ratio of openings to wall being strangely low.

Housing works well when there is clear definition of public and private space. Any ambiguity in this distinction can lead to potential problems. The architectural alchemy occurs in the design and quality of the ingredients that come together to create different territories. Budgets are always extremely tight in funded projects such as this, making it difficult to justify overindulging in the architectural specification of external spaces.

This dilemma is balanced well in Page + Park's Westerton Road project. The external surfaces and landscape are carefully considered. There are gardens and paths, play areas, a basketball court and communal external spaces. The urban form secures these public spaces within the elliptical form, making them spaces private to occupants. But the spaces don't have the charm of their 'fishing village' reference point. In a traditional fishing village, the intensity and proximity of buildings create a more potent kind of space, and accidental, undesigned elements occur within the village context. The ability to extend, paint and alter make it (in the village context) difficult for Westerton Road to compete visually with the source of its concept.

This is evidenced in the colour and materiality used by Page + Park. The hard and soft theme, brick to timber, and the colour choices don't work in the way they might in an older, more established coastal-village situation. It's too designed. Detailing is not complex, but the use of the materials and choice of colours leads the eye away from the power of the urban diagram in the sense that the strength of the project doesn't rely on colour or minor forced variation. This isn't helped by more idiosyncratic decisions, such as the tapering of gables or chamfering of corners, or splaying leading edges of roofs. There is a lot going on and, visually, this doesn't totally hang together in a controlled and coherent way, as is the case in the urban diagram.

Just how Page + Park managed to execute so many ideas within the budget is nothing short of miraculous. For £3.1 million the firm has provided 52 housing units, with little or no repetition of house type and a substantial common room and support-staff accommodation building. The site layout is high on external wall area, which makes its construction within such a tight budget even more of an achievement.

Beyond this, the client and architects have together created a unique self-contained architectural housing entity within which an otherwise controversial social mix is working in a nonobtrusive dignified way, where people openly and warmly tell you how much they love their homes, and where they feel secure and safe.

Page + Park Architects appreciates the strength of its client's architectural awareness – the strength of its commitment to the integration of disenfranchised people into its projects. This mutual respect is reciprocated by the Loretto Housing Association through the structure of its briefing document, which sets out the association's housing mix and programmatic requirements yet avoids any attempt to influence or steer the architecture. In this way, the architects are given their place to conceptualise and think freely regarding how to interpret the site and brief.

Within its modest immediate context, Westerton Road sets a new standard in terms of how housing could be made. It highlights the ordinariness of much of our built environment, particularly the suburban. It is thought provoking and engaging, and a credit to its authors and client. ∆+

Henry McKeown is an architect and director of JM Architects (formerly McKeown Alexander Architects) Glasgow. He has built a number of award-winning social-housing projects in the city. He also works as a design tutor at the Mackintosh School of Architecture studio, working in the urban design and housing programme.

EXPRESSING MORE THAN STRUCTURE

Virginia Fairweather's critical appreciation of the work of Thornton-Tomasetti Engineers, *Expressing Structure: The Technology of Large-Scale Buildings*, presents more than the title suggests, say **Kate** and **Ian** Abley.

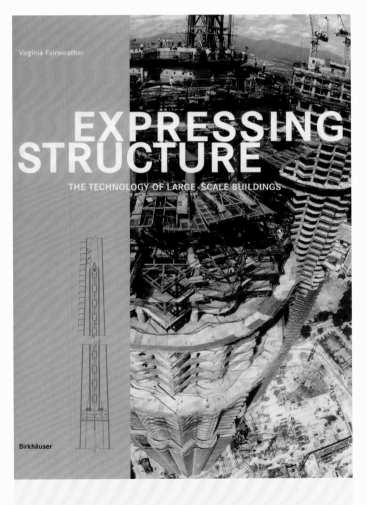

Expressing Structure is a gutsy read beyond the accounts of high-rise projects, such as the Skybridge between the Petronas Towers in Kuala Lumpur, Malaysia, and of large roof and long-span structures. Buildings with 'expressed structure', for Virginia Fairweather, are best designed 'with harmony between the structural system and the architectural form' (p 6). Over half a century, the featured practice, Thornton-Tomasetti Engineers (TT), has applied the latest building systems and materials technology to produce efficient interdisciplinary designs.[1]

It seems odd in a book subtitled *The Technology of Large-Scale Buildings* that little equivalent consideration is given to building services. We are told that while 'expressed structure is not always exposed structure … exposed structure is always expressed' (p 7). If the aim is to show 'how the building stands', why not reveal how the building works? (p 6) To be consistent then, not all 'expressed servicing' need be exposed. However, exposing ducts, pipes and wires is an irrational maintenance problem, and often plain ugly. Architecture, integrated with structure, is usually better when it contains and conceals servicing.

British architects and engineers have long been in the business of showing the guts of their buildings.[2] Despite a slow start, they have focused on integrated services too.[3] This was taken to a stunning extreme by Sir Richard Rogers in his Lloyds of London building in 1986. Rogers has since sophisticated his theory of expression in practice, recommending 'legibility' in the 2005 upgrade of the Richard Rogers Partnership (RRP) website: 'Work, leisure and domestic activities are becoming interchangeable, leading to the creation of open-ended, flexible structures … These buildings, with their legible facades and logical form, relate directly to both the user and passers-by.'[4]

Left

James Stirling and James Gowan, Leicester Engineering Building, University of Leicester, 1959–63
The engineering building both challenged the empty form-follows-function mantra of Functionalism and showed that Expressionism was possible without loss of either a strong form or clear function. Intended to accommodate change, protection as a Grade II* Listed Building has rendered it a burden on the university estate.

Right

Richard Rogers Partnership, Lloyds Building, London, 1978–86
The Lloyds Building is either loved or hated. The work of RRP has developed this theme in several schemes since, but never again to the extent to which the building services were exposed to the elements in this classic of 'high tech' styling.

Flexibility may be rhetorical. Legibility assumes the public wants to relate to the building. In the case of the 30 St Mary Axe headquarters for Swiss Re by Foster and Partners,[5] the concealed but nonetheless expressed structure engineered by Arup is easy on the eye and encourages the curious.[6] The prefabricated steel-and-glass cupola is a triumph developed by Waagner Biro.[7] The building services function with the building form. In passing from 'high tech', which was invariably a misnomer, to 'sustainable', which defies definition, Expressionist designers now tend to keep the guts on show, but inside – the Apple approach, but without the R&D of product design.

Such design subtlety in construction has a learning curve spanning careers and countless staff, as Fairweather clearly shows. Architects and engineers of one-off buildings need a series of collaborations to develop their modular aesthetic in a process spanning clients.

Fairweather's one-sidedness towards structure is immediately forgiven, because she theorises about design in one practice, implicitly in an age of popular environmentalism, and explicitly after the attack on the World Trade Center in New York on 11 September 2001. She appreciates that today there is a 'contentious array of parties' with different stakes in every large project. In response, she suggests that 'every participant on the design team must be consummately tactful' (p 10), by which she means that 'advancing the design requires that all participants on the team be sensitive to the issues the others are considering' (p 8).

The recurring theme for Fairweather is tact. Similarly, back in 1977, noting that specialisation in construction was the passing of the 'pristine audacity of the Renaissance Man',[8] W Houghton-Evans and Herbert Wilson wrote in the *Architects' Journal Handbook of Building Structure* that: 'Engineering and architecture confront one another as estranged members of a once-united family. During their long years apart they have acquired strange habits, and, if there is to be renewed

association, patience, tact and understanding will be called for on both sides.'[9]

We disagree.

Famous as a hard-fought collaborative design between Richard Rogers, Renzo Piano, Ted Happold and Peter Rice, the Centre Pompidou in Paris was also opened in 1977.[10] An obvious modular megastructure, Beaubourg was conceived as a legible and flexible serviced structural framework that is never architecturally finished and, at least theoretically, allowed for expansion or contraction. Since then, collaborative working has become conventional, with 'tactfulness' seen as an important virtue in construction. But tact can mean different things to different people.

According to the *Chambers Dictionary*, tact means 'managing the feelings' of others, which is diplomacy at best, but therapy at worst.[11] Decisive and insightful design involves tact, but also confrontation where necessary. Fairweather notes that hierarchical organisation is out. The institutionalised promotion of teamwork in construction considers leadership elitist and adversarial. Teamworking, in America it seems as much as in Britain, is about therapeutic forms of management that expect compromise from everyone in the process of getting buildings built.[12] Tact has been gutted.

It is true that 'building an "irrational" design can cost a lot of money' (p 8). Robust individuals need to challenge the irrationalities of colleagues, other specialists or clients, in the expectation that the favour will be reciprocated. This is because interdisciplinary design harmony is not created through compromise, but conflict. Design expression can spin off on tangents, views can differ significantly, and people can be wrong. Form and function are locked in a dynamic tension that can result in the blossoming of both, as far as the

Below
Foster and Partners, Swiss Re Headquarters, 30 St Mary Axe, London, 2004
The Swiss Re Building has an expressed structure of diagonal steel, held in tension at the nodes, and concealed with a lining that can be seen through the spiralling cladding that follows the superb atria spaces within. The structural approach could have efficiently scaled up to greater building height and volume, except for the institutionalised nervousness about building big in the capital city of 'Little Britain'.

project circumstances will allow.[13] The 'creative process can be hard work indeed' (p 10). Fairweather blames professional specialisation for 'less than optimal designs' (p 6). However, the division of labour is not at fault.

Commercial and regulatory circumstances are never of a consultant's choosing, and tact also means 'doing exactly what is the best in the circumstances'.[14] Today, the construction industry lacks individuals with what is presently perceived as the tactlessness to advance development through personality and daring. It needs people to challenge the circumstances on offer – characters like Lev Zetlin, the founder of Lev Zetlin Associates in 1956, which later became Thornton-Tomasetti, who Richard Tomasetti remembers 'had guts', and who forced his staff to follow his lead (p 12). The point is that circumstances need not be tactfully accepted.

The scope for development is being narrowed, not just by clients and regulators, but often by consultants too. *Expressing Structure* shows that there are serious technical challenges in building tall, long and wide. But more problematic is when individuals lack the confidence to stand by their own ideas and abilities, to give and receive criticism. There are too many people hiding in the apparent safety of any consensus that interdisciplinary meetings arrive at over insecure imponderables, like 'Is this building sustainable?', or 'Is this building safe from terrorist attack?'

Such diffusion can clearly be seen in the way that Rogers explodes collaborative design into 'participatory procedures', involving 'all the key stakeholders of a project',[15] hoping to design ' "natural" means of achieving benign environmental conditions … working with the climate, rather than trying to defeat it'.[16] Similarly, Tomasetti has contributed the chapter 'Protective Design of Structures' to *Building Security: Handbook for Architectural Planning and Design*, which is styled as 'the definitive 21st-century reference on security design, technology, building operations and disaster planning.'[17]

Beaubourg looked forward to social change, even as environmentalism was becoming orthodoxy. Rogers has reinterpreted his modular expression of structure and services as sustainable development. The engineering of

Thornton-Tomasetti before 9/11 was not justified in anticipation of terrorism. Architectural and engineering design expresses the dominant idea of the age. Both RRP and TT will continue to produce expressive buildings, but tact requires that they express the contemporary sense of exaggerated vulnerability to natural or man-made hazards.

In *Expressing Structure*, Virginia Fairweather encourages architects and engineers to continue to collaborate to harmonise form and function. But doing so fully requires a show of guts – and we don't mean the guts of their buildings. △+

Notes
1 www.thettgroup.com, accessed 06/05/05
2 James S Russell, 'Introduction', in *Pioneering British 'High-Tech'*, Phaidon (London), 1999, from the '3 Architectures' series that reprinted titles from the 'Architecture in Detail' series: John McKean, James Stirling and James Gowan, *Leicester University Engineering Building 1959–63*, Phaidon (London), 1994; Gabriele Bramante, *Foster Associates – Willis Faber & Dumas Building Ipswich 1975*, Phaidon (London), 1993; Kenneth Powell, *Richard Rogers Partnership – Lloyds Building 1978–86*, Phaidon (London), 1994.
3 Reyner Banham, *The Architecture of the Well-Tempered Environment*, University of Chicago Press, 2nd edn, 1984. First published 1969.
4 www.richardrogers.co.uk, accessed 04/05/05.
5 www.fosterandpartners.com, accessed 06/05/05.
6 www.arup.com, accessed 06/05/05.
7 www.waagner-biro.at, accessed 06/05/05.
8 W Houghton-Evans and Herbert Wilson, 'Building Structure: General', in Allan Hodgkinson (ed), *AJ Handbook of Building Structure*, Architectural Press (London), 2nd edn, 1977, p 2.
9 Ibid, p 7.
10 Nathan Silver, *The Making of Beaubourg: A Building Biography of the Centre Pompidou, Paris*, MIT Press (Cambridge, MA), 1994.
11 *The Chambers Dictionary*, Chambers Harrap Publishers (Edinburgh), 1999. First published 1901.
12 James Woudhuysen, Ian Abley, Stefan Muthesius and Miles Glendinning, *Why is Construction So Backward?*, Wiley (Chichester), 2004. Further details at www.audacity.org.
13 Reyner Banham, *Theory and Design in the First Machine Age*, Architectural Press (London), 1997. First published 1960.
14 *The Chambers Dictionary*, op cit.
15 www.richardrogers.co.uk, accessed 04/05/05.
16 Richard Rogers, 'Towards Sustainable Architecture: Environmental Research and Development at RRP', www.richardrogers.co.uk, accessed 04/05/05.
17 Richard L Tomasetti and John Abruzzo, 'Protective Design of Structures', in Barbara A Nadel (ed), *Building Security: Handbook for Architectural Planning and Design*, American Institute of Architects (New York), 2005.

Virginia Fairweather, *Expressing Structure: The Technology of Large-Scale Buildings,* Birkhauser Verlag AG (Basel, Berlin, Boston), December 2004; ISBN 3764366664.

Kate Abley is director of www.audacity.org. Ian Abley is an architect, co-author (with James Woudhuysen) of *Why is Construction so Backward?* (Wiley-Academy, 2004) and co-editor (with Jonathan Schwinge) of the Jan/Feb 2006 edition of *△*, entitled *Man-Made Modular Megastructures* – see inside back cover for further details.

McLean's Nuggets

Proposed temporary Tensairity™ bridge showing load capacity.

Air Bubbles

Interest in air structures continues to expand. The air-filled pillows of Vector-Foiltec's ethylene tetra fluoro ethylene (ETFE) head for world domination (global markets) with the pioneer spirit of architect/innovator Ben Morris after the recent announcement that the Swiss Birds Nest of Beijing's 2008 Olympic stadium and the adjacent bubble-filled envelope for the competition pool will be clothed in hectares of the stuff. Elsewhere, the structural possibilities of pneumatic structures are again being explored. Swiss inflatables firm Airlight Ltd has trademarked a new pneumatic technology entitled Tensairity™, which uses a combination of low-/medium-pressure air beams, helical cabling and struts inspired by the tensegrity/floating compression structures of Buckminster Fuller and artist Kenneth Snelson. These new lightweight composite beams have been proposed as bridge structures, temporary enclosures and wide-span roofs. In Luchsinger's and Perdetti's paper outlining Tensairity's structural principles and the field of pressure-induced stability, the technology is said to be capable of the load bearing of a steel beam, with substantial weight reduction. Meanwhile, at Per Lindstrand's West of England's Oswestry base, Lindstrand Technologies continues to grow alongside the aviators' erstwhile hot-air balloon business. It has recently completed a variety of 'blow-ups' that include an aircraft hangar for the Ministry of Defence and Swedish air force, a 50-metre-high transparent cone in Oberhausen, Germany, and an inflatable touring exhibition building – 'Thought Bubbles' – for the Welsh Development Agency. Interestingly, one of the most comprehensive catalogues of pneumatic structures is still Cedric Price's 1971 HMSO report *Air Structures: A Survey Commissioned by the Ministry of Public Building and Works*. Listed as a reference in the report is the lightweight structures pioneer and pneumatics advocate, current Royal Institute of British Architects (RIBA) Gold Medallist Frei Otto.

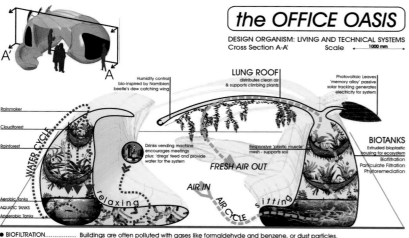

the OFFICE OASIS

DESIGN ORGANISM: LIVING AND TECHNICAL SYSTEMS
Cross Section A-A'   Scale |——1000 mm——|

LUNG ROOF
distributes clean air & supports climbing plants

Humidity control bio-inspired by Namibian beetle's dew catching wing

Photovoltaic Leaves 'memory alloy' passive solar tracking generates electricity for system

Rainmaker
Cloudforest
Rainforest

WATER CYCLE

Drinks vending machine encourages meetings plus: 'dregs' feed and provide water for the system

Responsive 'plastic muscle' mesh - supports soil

BIOTANKS
Extruded bioplastic housing for ecosystem
Biofiltration
Particulate Filtration
Phytoremediation

FRESH AIR OUT

AIR IN

AIR CYCLE

relaxing   sitting

Aerobic Tanks
AQUATIC TANKS
Anaerobic Tanks

- ● BIOFILTRATION............... Buildings are often polluted with gases like formaldehyde and benzene, or dust particles. In the Biotanks microoragnisms transform pollutants into harmless byproducts.
- ● OXYGEN PRODUCTION.... Cycling of air through diverse ecosystems produces oxygen by photosynthesis. Hollow tubes in Lung Roof distribute oxygenated fresh air onto individuals in the Oasis.
- ● ENERGY SYSTEMS........... Internal pumps are powered by pivoting Photovoltaic Leaves.
- ● MATERIALS..................... Main structure is assembled from extruded biodegradeable polymers, with recycled polythene lining.
- ● HUMAN SYSTEMS............. Lounging and seating areas for public or intimate interaction, observation of nature and enjoying refreshments.

Biomimetics (Keeping It Crispy)

The ever-developing field of biomimetics continues to produce a refreshingly analogical approach to engineering, not in its zoomorphic appropriation (Calatrava's overwrought structures or the more succinct giant prawns of Morecambe previously brought to you by that illusive trio Birds Portsmouth Russum), but by the analogy of the mechanism itself. This useful distillation of complex organisms, operations and properties into engineering questions seems entirely logical. At a recent event at the University of Westminster, Professor Julian Vincent (Director of the Centre for Biomimetic and Natural Technologies at the University of Bath) talked of the aeroelastic structure of the dragonfly's wing, the bistable structures of a lizard's tongue or retractable tape measure, and analysis of the walking biped, which took in Jacques Tati's

Cross-section through the Office Oasis by John-Paul Frazer/Exergy Ltd.

Invisible Cloak showing how to see through someone.

Suited and Rebooted

Thank goodness for *Future Materials*, the textiles trade magazine, whose recent round-up of 'intelligent' textiles has revealed a virtual wardrobe full of technology-rich apparel. My summary includes: nano-coated trousers that repel stains and extend durability; speedy swimsuits in fabrics modelled with computational fluid dynamic (CFD) analysis to emulate the denticles of sharkskin; and self-ironing shirts that use shape memory alloy (SMA) technology with titanium woven within a fabric matrix. The SMAs enable the shirt to remember its predesigned creases. Most enigmatic is the Invisible Cloak designed by Susumu Tachi, Professor of Computer Science and Physics at Tokyo University. The cloak is part of a range of 'optical camouflage' being developed by Tachi Labs, which uses a camera, computer, projector and a retroreflective material. This material, which is also used for traffic signs and other 'high visibility' products, only reflects light in the same way from which it has come, thus the 'cloaked' objects are invisible only from one viewpoint. While this technology at the level of apparel has certain logistical problems, its proposed uses include a transparent cockpit floor for the safe landing of aircraft, and a transparent rear of a car for road safety. Perhaps its use could be extended into the built environment for the selective visual removal of buildings. If Professor Tachi's cloak fails to reduce your visual impact, then Fuji has developed 'Wonderslim' underwear that uses coated fibres containing seaweed and caffeine, activating fat-dissolving enzymes; add to this socks that improve oxygenation for diabetics and a litany of wearable motherboards and solar-powered jackets and you begin to get an insight into the rapidly developing field of 'technical textiles'. One company working in this field is Ayrshire-based Culzean Textile Solutions whose development work includes a cosmic dust-resistant space tether for satellite recovery, a textile-reinforced suspension spring for London taxis, new knitted 3-D spacer fabrics (a technical panacea) for the composites industry, and the technology to knit a bifurcated artificial artery (aorta) as a medical product. 'We weave and knit everything except clothing' is an accurate slogan from a firm that acts as a technical laboratory for clients as diverse as construction, healthcare and the automotive industry. ⌀+

overbalanced (ready to go) pose and Groucho Marx's subvention of walking etiquette (in engineering terms), and ended with a preview of current research into the 'crispness of crisps'. Evidently, the fissure in a just-crunched potato crisp travels at an astonishing 300 metres per second, which in a good-quality potato chip will produce sparks if eaten in a darkened room. Designer John-Paul Frazer's Bioinspiration (www.bioinspiration.com) uses a biomimetic approach whereby 'architectural and product designs are inspired by nature': passive air-conditioning for a luxury hotel in India inspired by the self-regulating temperature control of a termite mound and the Office Oasis (see illustration) with Jacques Ableman described as a design organism. This prototypical study of human comfort and local climate control in the work place includes air and water treatment and energy production, demonstrating the technologies and processes of photosynthesis, photovoltaics, anaerobic and aerobic digestion, biofiltration and the utilisation of biodegradable polymers. Frazer is also about to launch Exergy, a website specialising in environmentally benign products.

'McLean's Nuggets' is an ongoing technical series inspired by Will McLean and Samantha Hardingham's enthusiasm for back issues of ⌀, as explicitly explored in Hardingham's ⌀ issue *The 1970s is Here and Now* (March/April 2005).

Will McLean is joint coordinator (with Pete Silver) of technical studies in the Department of Architecture at the University of Westminster, and is currently collaborating with artist Bruce McLean and architects David Watts and Irene Farish of North Ayrshire Council, on a new primary school under construction in Dalry, Scotland.

Jean Nouvel's exterior for Hotel Puerta América features a multicoloured array of panels inscribed with extracts from *Liberty*, a poem by Paul Eluard, in various languages.

PUERTA OF DREAMS

Howard Watson reviews the designs for Hotel Puerta América, a hotel in which every signature architect has had his or her hand. However, will it render Madrid the new Barcelona?

Foster, Hadid, Chipperfield, Gluckman, Pawson and Arad all working on the same building? The Silken Group certainly doesn't lack ambition. It has invested 75 million euros and hired 18 of the world's leading architects and designers to create an iconic 360-room hotel for Madrid. The group's president claims that Hotel Puerta América is: 'A project where acclaimed architects and designers have conveyed their dreams to us. It is a homage to the world of architecture, design and to freedom.' Rarely is quite so much expectation placed upon a commercially financed project, but the reasons go beyond the cast of superstar architects and the level of investment.

The word 'freedom' is not used glibly: the hotel plays a very demonstrative part in Madrid's rehabilitation after the terrible rail bombings of 2004. That year was meant to be a milestone in the city's tourism, following massive investment in its major museums. Madrid has long lagged behind Barcelona both in terms of significant architecture and self-promotion, and has appeared to be ignorant of the hotel-design renaissance that has helped re-energise tourism in many European cities. At the point at which Madrid was finally awakening, the rail

bombings put it in trauma. Puerta América isn't just a place for the daydreams of architects and night-dreams of residents: it has the frightening responsibility of being a highly publicised crucible for a city's rebirth.

Silken calls Puerta América the first multicultural hotel project in Spain, with designers originating from both Americas, Asia, Australia and all over Europe. It's a who's who of modern architecture, and with different designers for each of the 12 storeys it is inevitably a dictionary of different styles. In fact, Silken was not seeking any cohesion between the floor designs, asking the designers not to talk to each other. Apart from dealing with so many distinctive egos (surely one of the most formidable tasks in the history of project management), one of the main issues was to create a meaningful box for such a compendium. Jean Nouvel designed the exterior, and he chose to address directly the principal themes of internationalism and freedom. The facade is made up of blocks of colour, rising up through orange to yellow, and down to deep terracotta

Below
The hotel has 12 storeys, each featuring interiors by different architects and designers, including Jean Nouvel, Norman Foster, Zaha Hadid, Richard Gluckman, Estudio Mariscal, Ron Arad, Marc Newson and Arata Isozaki

and purple. These coloured panels are studded with excerpts from Paul Eluard's poem *Liberty*, written in many languages including French, English, Chinese and Arabic (and thereby holding a memory of the Islamic use of calligraphy). Freedom, democracy and inclusiveness are ingrained in the design.

Inside, Puerta América is a hotchpotch, but the problem is lessened by using the arch-minimalist John Pawson to design the communal areas, creating a passive backdrop to the chaos of themes that inhabit the rooms on different floors. A few architecture critics have claimed that some of the more famous contributors have merely placed their signature style within a hotel context. It seems that if the hotel conveys the designers' dreams, then some critics can only wish insomnia upon them. Having so many contributors, it is difficult to like everything about Puerta América, but by the same token it is hard not to find many things that are delightful. It is refreshing that it is some of the lesser-known contributors who have teased out innovation among the company of giants.

London-based Plasma, for instance, has thrown the book out of the window, breaking down the typical linearity of hotel structures by creating a fourth-floor corridor with a stainless-steel skin that contorts along angular planes and fractures according to its own rhythm. The steel reflects seams of coloured light that change along the course of the corridor and identify a zonal colour code that seeps into the rooms. The floor is not a comfort zone, but rather a realignment of

Inside, Puerta América is a hotchpotch, but the problem is lessened by using the arch-minimalist John Pawson to design the communal areas, creating a passive backdrop to the chaos of themes that inhabit the rooms on different floors. A few architecture critics have claimed that some of the more famous contributors have merely placed their signature style within a hotel context.

Top
Eva Castro and Holger Kehne of Plasma have used fractured planes and coloured neon to subvert the expectations and regimentation of hotel corridor and room design.

Bottom
With an emphasis on stone and water, the foyer is designed by John Pawson to be a curving, cloister-like space.

From different viewpoints, it is easy to be embarrassed by the way Puerta América literally wears its heart on its sleeve, or to be tempted to write it off as a huge marketing ploy. Nevertheless, among all the philosophical extemporising, it does follow through its intent to stand tall for democratic, inclusive principles, and among the sensational publicity there are many innovative design gems to behold. ∆+

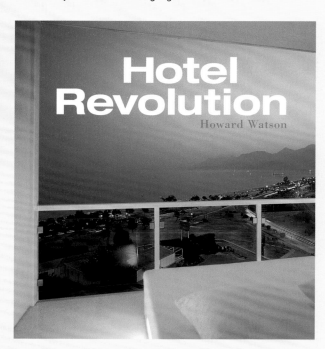

identity in a surreal, nonrepetitive space. On the eighth floor, which was designed by Kathryn Findlay, British lighting designer Jason Bruges offers another invigorating idea of identity within the hotel space. The corridor walls are lined with sensors that trace the guests' movements. The images are then absorbed and edited to form a shadow play that develops through the course of the day: the guests become part of the hotel design.

Some of the old masters have also stepped up to the challenge, particularly Ron Arad whose seventh-floor rooms feature a central, flowing mass that belches out the utilities and removes the need for internal barriers. Even if the work of other contributors is unlikely to be classed as experimental, it will still be fresh to most of the guests as they are unlikely to have experienced the signature style of the likes of Pawson and Foster within a more-or-less domestic setting.

Howard Watson is the author of *Bar Style: Hotels and Members' Clubs* (Wiley-Academy, 2005). He is currently writing *Hotel Revolution: 21st-Century Hotel Design*, also in the 'Interior Angles' series, which reassesses the diversity of hotel design in the wake of the boutique hotel.